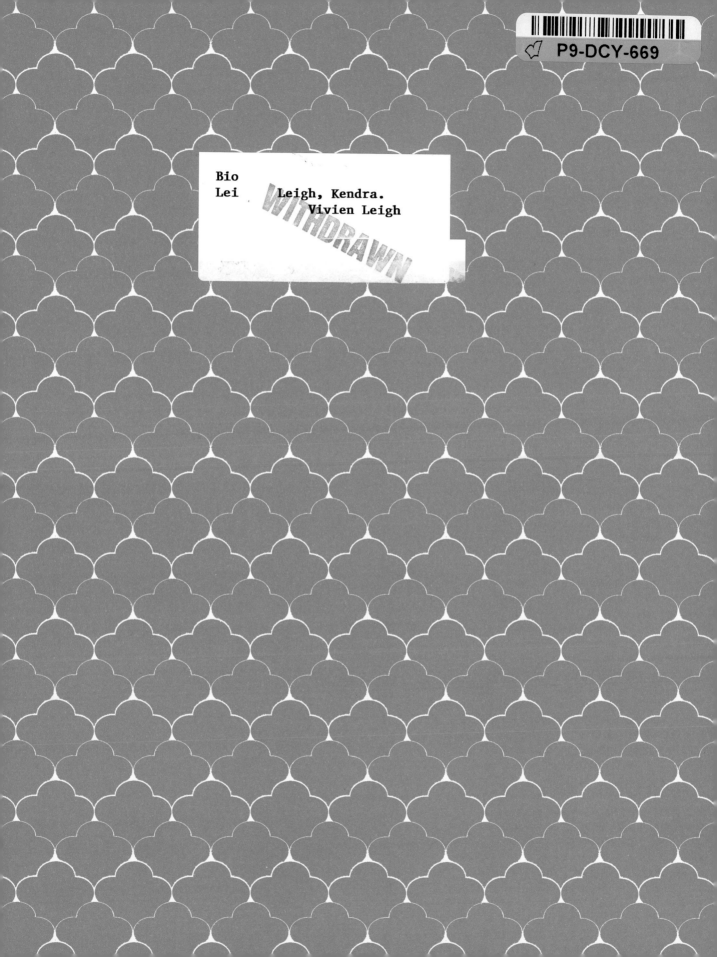

VIVIEN LEIGH

AN INTIMATE PORTRAIT

VIVIEN LEIGH

AN INTIMATE PORTRAIT

KENDRA BEAN

RUNNING PRESS
PHILADELPHIA · LONDON

Books published by Running Press are available at special discounts for bulk
purchases in the United States by corporations, institutions, and other organizations.
For more information, please contact the Special Markets Department at the
Perseus Books Group, 2300 Chestnut Street, Suite 200, Philadelphia, PA 19103,
or call (800) 810-4145, ext. 5000, or e-mail special.markets@perseusbooks.com.

ISBN 978-0-7624-5099-2
Library of Congress Control Number: 2013936755

E-book ISBN 978-0-7624-5103-6

9   8   7   6   5   4   3   2   1
Digit on the right indicates the number of this printing

Designed by Joshua McDonnell
Edited by Cindy De La Hoz
Typography: Avenir, Bembo, and Lato

Running Press Book Publishers
2300 Chestnut Street
Philadelphia, PA 19103-4371

Visit us on the web!
www.runningpress.com

FOR MOM, DAD, AND DEREK

CONTENTS

FOREWORD BY CLAIRE BLOOM

I hold in my hand an antique enameled box, decorated with roses both inside and out. Fragile and exquisite, it was a gift to me from Vivien Leigh. I treasure it. Vivien chose her gifts with great care throughout the year, saving them for some special occasion and for the perfect recipient.

We met when performing together on the London stage in *Duel of Angels*, written by Jean Giraudoux. I was Lucrece, the sacrificial victim,

dressed in white. Vivien, dressed in red, was the dangerous and destructive Paola. This, the late '50s, was still the time of stylish theater, when leading ladies were expected to be both beautiful and beautifully dressed on and off the stage. Christian Dior designed our dresses. Vivien's beauty was like that of a Siamese cat, her eyes the same extraordinary shade of blue, her light movements almost feline in their grace. Her frame was so minute that when, in the course of the play, I put my arm around her shoulder, I felt I was embracing an exotic and fragile bird. And in a way, that is what she was.

I was eighteen years younger than my fellow actress, a difference in age that never once interfered with the great affection we developed for each other. Neither did the fact that I'd had a momentary dalliance with her husband, Laurence Olivier, when I acted opposite him in the film of *Richard III*. She could have resented this, she could have resented my youth; she never did.

The critical reviews of her performances were sometimes dismissive, once or twice downright insulting, as some thought it was impossible that someone so widely acknowledged as the most beautiful woman of her time could also be a fine and serious actress. Her performance as Cleopatra, her powerful and driven Lady Macbeth, above all the glorious Blanche in *Streetcar* were proof, if any were needed, that she was an important artist of both film and theater.

That there was a tragic side to her life only became clear to me during the run of the play. Once I visited her dressing room to find her in tears. I didn't know the reason, and didn't like to pry. But later I learned that rumors had reached her, hinting that Olivier had been seen dining after his show with pretty actresses a fraction of his age. The rumors turned out to be only too true.

Well and movingly described in this book, and certainly witnessed by others, are many accounts of her mental illness. Only once did I witness this most disciplined and dedicated actress in the grip of a terrible episode. I had left the play to appear in what I hoped might be an important film, *Look Back in Anger*. A few weeks later, at about three in the morning, I received a call from Vivien. She hadn't been well enough to appear in the play that night, and told me that she was at home, in her bath, and had tried to put her head under the water and drown herself. She was quite alone. Would I come over? I rushed into a taxi and arrived at Eaton Square. Far from being alone, Vivien was surrounded by a sea of people. A gramophone was playing at one end of the room, another playing some different record at the other. Vivien's beautiful face was swollen, almost unrecognizable. A doctor was trying to get her into the bedroom so he could inject her with some tranquilizer. I stayed for a while, until I realized there was absolutely nothing I could do.

After I quit the play, the close relationship that can be found only in the intimate setting of the theater faded, but never completely vanished. When my daughter was born a few years later, I had a loving telegram from Vivien: "Well done darling."

She loved those she loved with all her heart, and was loved unequivocally in return. I was lucky enough to have been accepted as a friend. That was no small privilege.

—Claire Bloom, April 2013

INTRODUCTION

When Vivien Leigh walked into a room, all eyes immediately fixed on her. This bewitching effect wasn't just because of her undeniable beauty. She had an aura—a magnetism that drew people in and left them spellbound. Her first love was for the stage, but her luminous intensity was magnified on the movie screen. Nearly half a century after physically departing this world, Vivien lives on in the film roles she made immortal. Whether clawing her way back to the top as civilization crumbled around her in *Gone With the Wind* or fighting and ultimately succumbing to harsh realities in *A Streetcar Named Desire*, Vivien had the unique power of immediacy which has kept her performances fresh—and thus helped keep her in the spotlight—long after many other stars of her generation have faded from memory.

Sir Alec Guinness, the great chameleon of British stage and screen, once said of her, "We have to love what we love, and we have to remain loyal. So many who loved Vivien's work—on the stage and on the screen—turned against it when

Vivien in character as Scarlett O'Hara.

she was frail or when the styles shifted from her corner. I can find no reasonable defense for this. We stand on shores every bit as slippery as Vivien's when we fail to honor our passions."

Like every public figure, Vivien had her detractors. Many were envious when she ran off with the most coveted role in film history. Thirty-three years after the fact, on *The Merv Griffin Show*, Bette Davis admitted she still held a grudge for not winning the role of Scarlett in *Gone With the Wind*. Others were quick to point out her learned, rather than natural, acting abilities. The emergence of renowned critic Kenneth Tynan onto the scene in the 1950s transformed Vivien from "a Queen who requires no consort" into a virtual moving target for criticism because she dared to act opposite the love of her life and her greatest mentor, who also happened to be England's Greatest Actor. But for every jealous barb thrown her way, for every negative review or misunderstood tantrum, there were ten people willing to stand up for her, to protect her, and to comfort her. "To know Vivien was to love her," Terence Rattigan eulogized in *The New York Times* on August 6, 1967. "To have loved Vivien was also to have been loved by her, and loved with a true devotion and a passionate loyalty that might well put your own wavering emotion to shame."

On the eve of her divorce from Laurence Olivier in 1960, Vivien gave voice to her anxieties about the future, writing to the man with whom she had spent twenty-five turbulent but in many ways rewarding years, "I hope my life will prove a useful and good one, to many people." This single quote seems to sum up the answer to a question that I have been asked several times since setting out to compile this book: Why does Vivien Leigh still matter?

I first became aware of her in *Gone With the Wind*. This seems to be the typical point of discovery for many fans, its wide availability and iconic status making it an easily accessible gateway into the world of classic Hollywood cinema. I can't remember a time in my life when I wasn't in love with the movies. As an impressionable teenager, the saga of Scarlett O'Hara struck a particular cord and I began devouring any literature I could get my hands on that would tell me more about the production and its stars. Out of the main players, Vivien emerged as the most interesting and enigmatic figure.

Despite being a consummate star, Vivien has managed to remain somewhat elusive. She never had the opportunity to pen her own story, and the most influential figure in her life, Laurence Olivier, consistently refused interviews with her many biographers. It was not until 1977, when Anne Edwards revealed Vivien's long-fought battle with manic depression (commonly referred to today as bipolar disorder), that the idyllic illusion surrounding Vivien and her marriage to Olivier was shattered.

The British Library's acquisition of Olivier's papers in 2000 has provided a unique lens through which to reassess the facets of Vivien's struggle with mental illness and her romantic and professional relationship with Olivier. This previously untapped treasure trove of archival material, which includes everything from personal correspondence between Vivien and Olivier to film contracts, doctor's notes, interview transcripts, and legal and medical records, sheds new light on these two topics that have been frequently discussed yet seemingly misunderstood.

It has been twenty-five years since the publication of the last significant Vivien Leigh biography. As she would have been one hundred years old in November 2013, it only seems fitting to bring her back into the spotlight by pairing new research with rare and previously unpublished photographs, showcasing her startling beauty, and conveying her multifaceted persona as a woman, an actress, and a legend.

London portrait photographer Vivienne (Florence Entwistle) said of Vivien, "She is an artist-photographer's dream and the fairest of the fair. Analyze her features—the proportion, the relationship of one to another, the harmony, the line. It is hard to fault them."

CHAPTER 1

FAME IN A NIGHT

"I saw her appearance in *The Mask of Virtue* at the Ambassadors Theatre—she was the loveliest thing I had ever seen on the stage."

—Isabel Jeans

Vivian Holman (née Hartley) was easily starstruck. She was eclectic in her tastes and enjoyed many hobbies, among them reading, collecting paintings, and gardening. Her favorite pastimes were going to the cinema and theater. Once under the spell of a certain performer, she was apt to see a particular film or play multiple times. It had always been this way. When she was seven years old and boarding at a convent school in Roehampton, she had begged her mother to take her into the city to see George Robey perform at the Hip-

podrome in Leicester Square. The "Prime Minister of Mirth" was her favorite actor and she saw *Round in 50* sixteen times. After seeing the 1929 MGM silent film *The Pagan*, Vivian fell in love with Mexican heartthrob Ramon Novarro.

In the mid-1930s, as the wife of a Middle Temple barrister, she could afford a good nanny for her baby daughter, Suzanne, with plenty of spending money left over to enjoy the leisurely pursuits London had to offer. It was no surprise then, that Vivian attended several performances of *Theatre Royal* in the autumn of 1934. George S. Kaufman and Edna Ferber's comedic parody of the real-life Barrymore clan was staged by Noël Coward at the Lyric The-

Vivian Mary Hartley, circa 1917.

As a child in India, Vivian's imagination flourished. When asked in 1960 why she initially wanted to become an actress, she said, "I like dressing up, I think."

atre in Shaftesbury Avenue. Playing hard-drinking womanizer Anthony Cavendish (a fictional John Barrymore) was Laurence Olivier, one of the most promising actors on the London stage. Olivier's brooding good looks and dynamic style were a heady combination. Vivian was a firm believer in fate. She sat with rapt attention as Olivier cavorted around the stage, and there, illuminated by the footlights, she saw her entire future. Turning to her girlfriend, Vivian suddenly whispered, "That's the man I'm going to marry." Startled, her friend reminded her that both she and Olivier were already married—to other people. "It doesn't matter," Vivian replied. "I'm still going to marry him one day." Little did she know that in a few short months, she herself would become the toast of the London theater scene in her first West End play. Her

name on the program would read Vivien Leigh.

Vivien was seven when she told her school friend Maureen O'Sullivan that she wanted to become an actress. It may have seemed a strange profession to choose at such a young age, particularly for a girl who grew up within the strict confines of convent life. But she was never one to adhere to convention. O'Sullivan, who later became famous for playing Jane opposite Johnny Weissmuller in the *Tarzan* films, remembered how, even as a child, Vivien flaunted an aura of individuality. "She was always a beautiful little girl. I remember we used to

do silly little things in school like voting for the most popular, or the most pretty, or the most talented, or the most likely to be outstanding in the world. And I remember Vivien Leigh got the vote. Vivien always wanted to be an actress. She was single-minded. She was the only girl in school to take ballet, for instance. She took it alone, the only one. I thought it was rather brave of her."

The seeds of imagination were planted in Darjeeling, India, where she was born Vivian Mary Hartley on November 5, 1913, the only child of Yorkshire-born stockbroker Ernest Richard Hartley and his wife, Gertrude Mary Frances. Later in life, Vivien would jokingly tell Laurence Olivier that she had been so spoiled as a child she believed the fireworks set off for Guy Fawkes Night were really in celebration of her birthday. Darjeeling was a popular vacation spot for British expats looking to escape the unbearable humidity of the Indian summer. For Vivien's mother, it held a spiritual quality. The story goes that Gertrude would often sit looking mesmerized at the distant Himalayas, in hopes that some of nature's great beauty would be passed to her unborn child.

In recent years, there has been speculation about Vivien's ancestral origins. Hugo Vickers revealed that her mother Gertrude might have been part Armenian or Parsee Indian, which would explain Vivien's "dark Eastern beauty." Gertrude's maiden name was Yackjee but she often went by the family name Robinson as a possible means of avoiding prejudice commonly displayed toward half-castes. Comparisons have been drawn between Vivien and actress Merle Oberon, who

Two portraits of Vivian taken by famed child photographer Marcus Adams in London, 1922.

starred in two films opposite Laurence Olivier and who was directly affected by xenophobic attitudes of the time. Throughout her adult life, she maintained that she'd been born in Tasmania, instead of Bombay, and that her Indian mother was not her mother at all. Oberon was signed to a film contract with Alexander Korda and went to great lengths to appear more "British." Such was not the case for Vivien, who never denied being born in India and whose exoticism was actually played up in the 1930s. Whatever her background, it didn't seem to have a negative impact on her life or career.

Vivien's flare for the dramatic likely came from her father. Along with polo and racing horses, Ernest enjoyed performing as an amateur member of the Calcutta Dramatic Society. Her mother was "the determined one in the family," according to Vivien. Gertrude instilled in her daughter a love of literature. Rudyard Kipling's *Just So Stories* was a particular favorite and Vivien made her mother continue to read them aloud despite knowing the words by heart. Vivien also delighted in the illusory worlds of Hans Christian Andersen, Lewis Carroll, and Greek mythology. Fantasy would be a recurring theme throughout her life, both in her work and the atmosphere she tried to create for other people.

In 1917, during the First World War, Ernest relocated to Bangalore and took up a job training horses for British troops fighting in the Middle East. His wife and daughter went to Ootacamund and continued to enjoy a privileged lifestyle. In nearby Mussoorie, three-year-old Vivien made her first appearance on stage. Jealousy broke out amongst the other children when she was chosen to play Bo Peep in a charity matinee of *Tom, Tom, the Piper's Son*. Vivien made an impression by announcing to the audience that instead of singing her song, she would recite it. Also in the show was Nancy Godden, whose sister Rumer would grow up to pen *Black Narcissus*. Rumer thought Vivien "a bewitching little girl."

Vivien's idyllic childhood came to an abrupt end in April 1920. Gertrude, a devout Roman Catholic, wanted her daughter to be raised in a religious environment. At age six, Vivien was taken back to England and deposited at the Convent of the Sacred Heart in Roehampton, West London. She wouldn't see her parents again for nearly two years. In the days of Empire, it was not uncommon for privileged parents living abroad to send their children "home" to receive their education. Several British actors of Vivien's generation, including Margaret Lockwood, Dulcie Gray, Googie Withers, and Basil Rathbone had similar experiences. It is conceivable that the feeling of abandonment Vivien experienced when left at the convent contributed to her eventual problematic behavior. Jack Merivale, Vivien's companion late in life, alluded to the uneasy relationship she had with Gertrude in later years. He said he "knew things were bad when she called for her mother." Gertrude lived in a state of denial about the mental health issues Vivien later suffered from and remained fiercely loyal, despite often being used as "a sort-of kicking board" during Vivien's bad times.

Vivien was the youngest pupil at the school and at least one classmate felt "there was an air of romance about this lovely little girl alone without her parents." Her friend Patricia (Patsy) Quinn (Lady Lambert) described her impression of Vivien to Alan Dent in 1969: "I can see her now—so tiny and delicately made, with wonderful large blue eyes

ABOVE: Vivian Hartley on her wedding day, December 20, 1932.

TOP RIGHT: The newly married Vivian and Herbert Leigh Holman, St. James's Roman Catholic Church, Spanish Place, London.

RIGHT: Vivian and Leigh Holman.

and chestnut wavy hair nearly to her waist—the tiny retroussé nose, and the only complexion I have ever seen that really *was* like a peach." Another fellow boarder, Jane Glass, recalled how Vivien was "cossetted and pampered by the nuns because her parents were in India—in those days like having parents on Mars." During holidays Vivien was often left behind while her friends rejoined their families. In an effort to soothe her loneliness, the Mother Superior allowed Vivien to take a white kitten to bed with her. Over time, Vivien adjusted to her surroundings, although the feeling of homesickness never dissipated entirely. In her letters home, she often expressed her wish to be "grown up" so that she could rejoin her parents.

For Vivien, convent life was a paradoxical mixture of order and rebellion. She found security in the strict daily routine of prayers and piety, but showed a tendency to defy authority. As she grew older, the nuns found they had "a real pickle" on their hands. Once when she was eleven, Vivien wrote home to report that Mother Brace-Hall had wished "tribulation" upon her: "She said it would do me a lot of good and that my friends wished I had it." There were threats of discipline but they were seldom enacted. Vivien was willful and learned quickly how to get what she wanted.

One of the most significant attributes she developed at school was her ability to make friends. In an effort to please her peers, Vivien kindly offered to share the fashionable gifts her parents sent over from India. Once she asked her mother to send a present for her friend Libby who had been "so disappointed at not getting any pearls." Although not very studious, Vivien enjoyed history and gravitated toward performing arts, tak-

ing up piano, violin, and playing the cello in the school orchestra. She also took part in a few student productions, playing the fairy Mustardseed in *A Midsummer Night's Dream*, Miranda in *The Tempest*, and the Golfing Girl in a play called *Ask Beccles*. She wasn't very successful in any of them. Her high-pitched voice didn't project beyond the first row and she forgot her lines. According to Hugo Vickers, "Bridget Boland, the child producer, taught her a sound lesson by hitting her over the head . . . with a candlestick."

Vivien left Roehampton in the summer of 1927 and spent the next five years cultivating her cosmopolitan image at a series of finishing schools on the continent. She became fluent in French and German. In Paris, she took elocution lessons with Mademoiselle Antoine, an actress with the Comédie-Française who encouraged trips to the Parisian theater. Her school in Bavaria offered plenty of opportunity for cultural excursions to nearby Vienna and Salzburg, but its main purpose was to prepare girls for a future of domesticity: "That meant that, being a girl, I *had* to learn What Every Hausfrau Should Know. And hated it," Vivien said in 1939. "That was one of the things that helped me make up my mind to become an actress."

At age eighteen, Vivien emerged from one type of education and stepped right into another. She auditioned and was accepted into London's Royal Academy of Dramatic Art. According to Felix Barker's authorized biography *The Oliviers*, published in 1953, Vivien's instructors at RADA thought she held great promise. Vivien remembered it differently in a 1961 interview: ". . . In fact, all my reports from the Academy were very bad. I did a play called *Caesar's Wife*, by Somerset Maugham, and I remember the report saying, 'Why are you so bad? Is it because you have too much sense of humor?' Well I don't know what the reason was, but I was very shocking. I expect I didn't concentrate." Yet, she was serious about pursuing what had become a great passion and neither marriage nor motherhood could deter her.

Vivien met barrister Herbert Leigh Holman, from whom she would borrow her stage name, at the South Devon Hunt Ball in 1931. He was thirteen years older than her and bore a strong resemblance to the actor Leslie Howard. Holman came from an old family, providing Vivien with the means to better her position and to develop an air of

sophistication and taste that would remain with her for the rest of her life. They married in December 1932 and the following year Vivien gave birth to their daughter, Suzanne. Motherhood did not come naturally. "I was not cast in the mold of serenity and in any case, although you may succeed in being kind at twenty you cannot be calm, with all your life still before you, and your ambitions unfulfilled," Vivien said. "I loved my baby as every mother does, but with the clear-cut sincerity of youth I realized that I could not abandon all thought of a career on the stage. Some force within myself would not be denied expression . . ."

Vivien's first professional acting job came in August 1934, when she was cast as a schoolgirl extra in the Gaumont British film *Things are Looking Up*, starring Cicely Courtneidge. Although her name didn't appear in the credits, she was singled out among the other extras because of her beauty and given one line of dialogue. Soon after, she signed with independent agent John Gliddon. He quickly found her roles in *Gentlemen's Agreement* and *The Village Squire*, two low-budget features distributed domestically by Paramount. Producer Anthony Havelock-Allan was in charge of casting both films. He didn't think Vivien a natural actress, but "thought that she was determined to be an actress. She wasn't happy in her situation and she wanted to improve it. She wanted a wider world to live in."

Vivien's next film was 1935's *Look Up and*

LEFT: One of several publicity photos taken of "Fame in a Night Girl" Vivien Leigh after the opening night of *The Mask of Virtue*, 1935.

RIGHT: Vivien Leigh became an overnight sensation playing Henriette Duquesnoy in *The Mask of Virtue*, 1935.

Laugh. She had a difficult time working with director Basil Dean, who showed little sympathy for her inexperience. Dean later wrote that Vivien had been "so uncontrollably nervous that for quite a while she seemed unable to take direction." But she found an ally in the film's star, Gracie Fields, who after a particularly difficult take offered the encouraging words, "Don't worry, love, you've *got* something." Afterward, Gliddon suggested Dean sign Vivien to a five-year contract with the recently formed Ealing Studios. Casting director Aubrey Blackburn liked the idea, but Dean decided she was "not yet a competent actress." Dean's short-sightedness about Vivien's potential set her on the path to stardom.

As darkness descended over London on May 15, 1935, an expectant crowd filled the intimate auditorium of the Ambassadors Theatre in Covent Garden. It was the opening night of theater impresario Sydney Carroll's latest production, *The Mask of Virtue.* Directed by Maxwell Wray and translated into English by Ashley Dukes, the play was produced specially for South African-born actress Jeanne de Casalis, with Frank Cellier and Lady Tree adding repute to the small cast. As the curtain rose on the comedy set in eighteenth-century France, the three established actors were largely forgotten as all eyes focused on the breathtaking vision in black lace standing at the back of the stage. Until then no one had heard of Vivien Leigh. By the next morning she was one of the most famous names in London.

"I remember the morning after *The Mask of Virtue* . . . that some critics saw fit to be as foolish as to say that I was a great actress," Vivien said in 1960. "And I thought that was a foolish, wicked thing to say, because it put such an onus and such

a responsibility onto me, which I simply wasn't able to carry."

She was in Fleet Street at four in the morning with her mother and Leigh Holman to catch the morning papers as they came off the press. The reviews were overwhelmingly positive, yet even in the elation of sudden fame, Vivien held no illusions as to why she had been cast as Henriette Duquensnoy. Sydney Carroll had been bowled over by her beauty when she and John Gliddon appeared at his office for a pre-audition meeting. The producer was famous for finding and exploiting new talent, and realized the potential that this new "discovery" could have for the success of his play. Her voice needed work, but Maxwell Wray praised her graceful movements and her ability to read lines with intelligence. Luckily, Vivien's established colleagues readily offered her support and guidance: "Every night I play in the theater I look at dear Lady Tree, who has spent so many wonderful years doing triumphantly what I am just trying to do with all my inexperience, my want of knowledge. I see beautiful Jeanne de Casalis holding the stage like its queen, and I worship Frank Cellier for showing me at every performance, how far I have to go before

TOP LEFT: *Fire Over England* (1937), the first film Vivien made for Alexander Korda. Pictured with American director William K. Howard.

LEFT: Vivien and Laurence Olivier as Cynthia and Michael in *Fire Over England*. Their real-life romance echoed in their onscreen performances.

TOP RIGHT: Hair modeling for Rudolph Steiner, 1936. Photo by Vivien's "official" photographer, Angus McBean.

RIGHT: A publicity portrait of Vivien as Victoria Gow in *Storm in a Teacup* (1937).

Picture Show, Vol. 28, No. 989   November 20th, 1937   Registered at the G.P.O. as a Newspaper

VIVIEN LEIGH
REX HARRISON & *"Scruffy"* in "STORM *in a* TEACUP

PICTURE SHOW

2d.
EVERY
TUESDAY

Vivien with Rex Harrison and Scruffy the dog for *Storm in a Teacup* (1937). Harrison was in love with Vivien, but "all she wanted to do was talk about Larry."

RIGHT: Vivien as Madeleine Goddard in *Dark Journey* (1937).

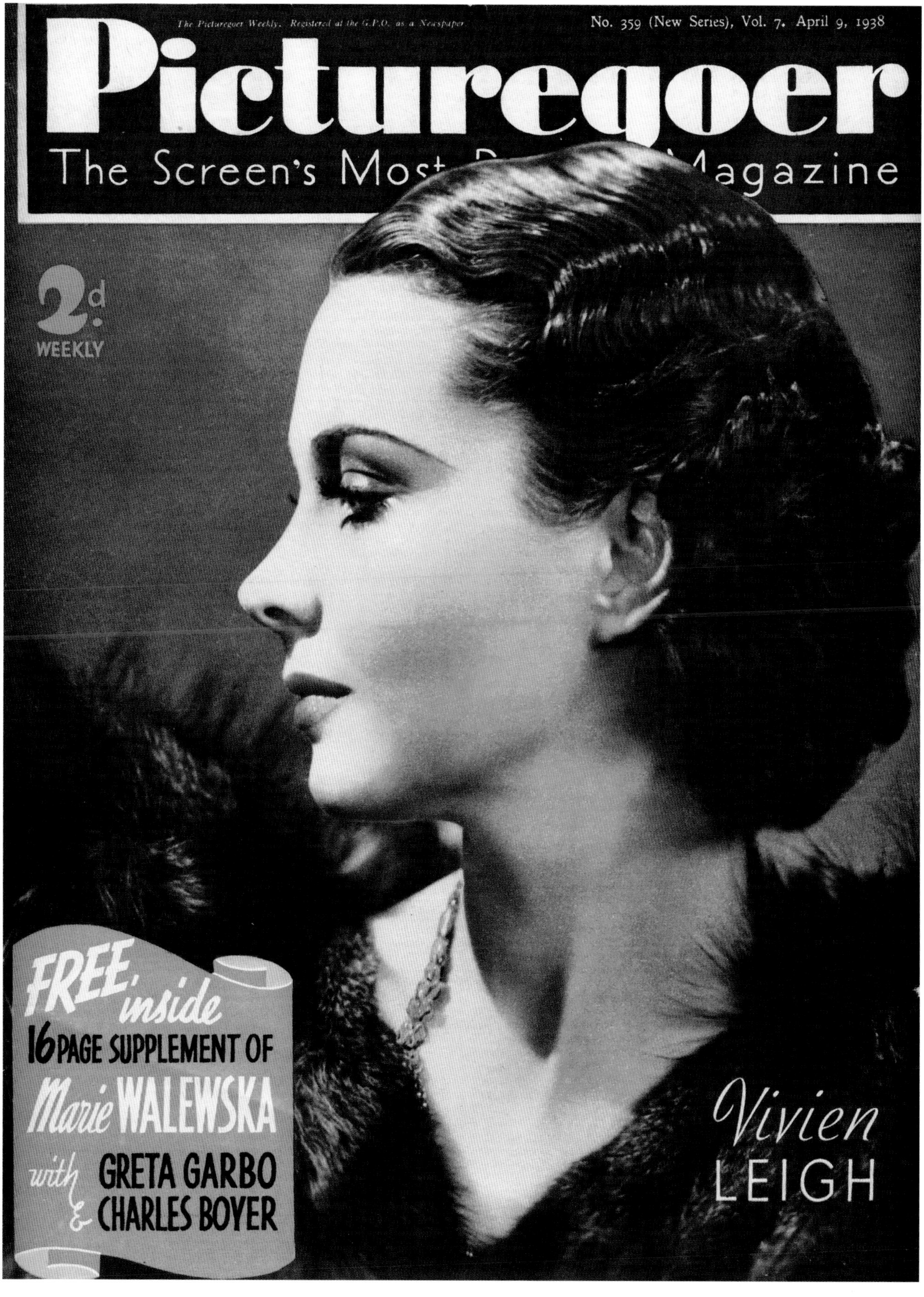

The Picturegoer Weekly. Registered at the G.P.O. as a Newspaper.
No. 359 (New Series), Vol. 7. April 9, 1938
Picturegoer
The Screen's Most
agazine
2d.
WEEKLY
FREE inside
16 PAGE SUPPLEMENT OF
Marie WALEWSKA
with GRETA GARBO
& CHARLES BOYER
Vivien
LEIGH

I can allow myself to think of myself as a real actress."

In the audience on the first night was film mogul Alexander Korda. Anthony Havelock-Allan maintained that the Hungarian producer was actually responsible not only for staging *The Mask of Virtue*, but also for casting Vivien. He told biographer Charles Drazin that Korda had seen Vivien in one of his earlier films and wanted to see if she could carry the play, "which she did." Whether or not this is true, Korda recognized Vivien's star quality to such a degree that he offered her a £50,000 film contract with an option to spend six months per year acting on stage.

Leigh Holman was asked to go over the legalities with Vivien and found the entire situation rather absurd. He didn't share his wife's interest in the performing arts, and therefore had misgauged the intensity of her ambition. At this stage in her career, Vivien was simply happy to be offered more chances to develop her craft. However, because her big break came on the stage rather than on the screen, she was able to align herself with the popular idea that theater was culturally superior to acting in films. It was an attitude common among classically trained actors of her generation, including Ralph Richardson, John Gielgud, and Laurence Olivier. In the Summer 1935 issue of *Theatre Illustrated Quarterly*, Vivien addressed her new fans: "One final word to theater folk. The films will never take me quite away from the stage . . . And the direct personal meeting with an audience means more to me than all the celluloid contacts in the world, whatever they mean in money and whatever they mean in fame."

Vivien's contract sat on the shelf at London

ABOVE: Basil Dean's "two joyful miscreants" on board the *Golden Eagle* for a river cruise to Southend during the filming of *21 Days Together* (1937). It was on this trip that Vivien told C. A. Lejeune that she intended to play Scarlett O'Hara.

TOP RIGHT: Vivien and Olivier lunching on the set of *21 Days Together* (1937).

BOTTOM RIGHT: Vivien and Olivier sit with costar Leslie Banks during a break from filming *21 Days Together* (1937).

ABOVE: With Olivier and Jill Esmond. Olivier's wife at the time he met Vivien. This is in Capri, 1936

RIGHT: Enjoying the sun in Capri, 1936.

FAR RIGHT: A tender moment between Vivien and Olivier in Capri, 1936.

Films for over a year while Korda was busy building Denham Studios. In the meantime, she continued to hone her experience on stage, acting with Ivor Novello and Marius Goring in Max Beerbohm's *The Happy Hypocrite*, and giving a performance as the Queen in an Oxford University Dramatic Society production of *Richard II*, directed by John Gielgud. Korda finally called on Vivien's services in the summer of 1936, casting her as Cynthia in the Elizabethan costume drama *Fire Over England*. In the role of her lover, Michael Ingolby, was Laurence Olivier.

Olivier had seen Vivien in *The Mask of Virtue* and immediately fell under the spell of her beauty,

ABOVE: Vivien as Wanda in *21 Days Together* (1937).

RIGHT: On the train to Denmark to perform in *Hamlet* with the Old Vic Company, June 1937.

although he confessed to not thinking much of her abilities as an actress at the time. Not long afterward, they formally met in the lobby of the Grill restaurant at the Savoy Hotel, a popular hot spot for London's theatrical society. Nearly a half-century later, Olivier could still recall exactly where Vivien had been sitting: "Except for seeing her on the stage, it was the first time I ever set eyes on that

Performing in *Hamlet* opposite Laurence Olivier at Kronborg Castle, Elsinore.

exquisite face. Yes, she saw me, too. But she was with a young man who looked very much in love, and I supposed that they were, to put it vulgarly, 'at it.'" The young man at Vivien's side was Gladys Cooper's son, John Buckmaster, with whom she was having a fling. Buckmaster annoyed Vivien by pointing at Olivier and commenting on how silly he looked without his mustache. "I was very indignant," Vivien recalled in 1960, "and I said rather pompously that he didn't look funny at all."

By the end of the evening, Olivier had invited Vivien and Leigh Holman to join him and his wife, Jill Esmond, for a weekend party at their house near Maidenhead. Subsequent run-ins followed sporadically—a luncheon here, a play there—until they met outside the canteen at Denham Studios on their first day of shooting and Vivien expressed to Olivier how nice it was that they'd be working together. Olivier supposedly replied, "We shall probably end up by fighting. People always get sick of each other when making a film." Instead, they began an illicit affair that would blossom into one of the most famed celebrity relationships of the twentieth century. Vivien later told Godfrey Winn, "I wonder whether—if the film was shown again—you would see it in our faces, the confrontation with our destiny. I don't think I have ever lived quite as intensely ever since. I don't remember sleeping, ever; only every precious moment that we spent together."

Fire Over England was intended as a vehicle for Flora Robson; however, Korda had his eye on advancing Vivien's career. As David O. Selznick would four years later, Korda began altering details of Vivien's life to fit with the star image he had in mind for her. She was marketed as an exotic, fashionable beauty, and details of her domestic life as a wife and mother were withdrawn from circulation. The British fan magazine *Picturegoer* felt "these were not desirable appendages for a young actress with her way to make in the great big world." In the same article, Vivien was quoted as boldly dismissing reports that her home life was more important than her desire for fame: "Rubbish, I don't know how that ever got into print."

Vivien's role in *Fire Over England* was minor, but she was promoted in publicity materials as one of the stars. Stills of her and Olivier embracing dominated the frame in several lobby cards and posters, indicating that Korda knew what was going on when the cameras stopped rolling and wanted to build them up as a prominent on-screen couple. Korda's encouragement of their real-life romance extended beyond the studio gates and he became a professional father figure to both Vivien and Olivier; a bond that lasted until his death in 1956.

Born in 1907 in Dorking, Surrey, Laurence Kerr Olivier was the youngest son of a parsimonious High Anglican priest who also made a "very frightening father figure." Like Vivien, events in his formative years had a lasting effect on his character. He was twelve when his beloved mother, Agnes, died of a brain tumor. She had been his "whole world" and he never got over her passing. As an adult he looked for devoted feminine affection in his choice of romantic partners. His father was distant, preferring religious fervor to compassion. Olivier felt unwanted as a child, which fostered in him a deep-seated insecurity. Guilt was also a constant bedfellow as a result of his religious upbringing. It was only when he stepped on stage at age ten while a

student at All Saints, Margaret Street, a boys' school near Oxford Circus, that he first felt a sense of importance. There was comfort in pretending to be someone else and throughout his career he subscribed to the idea of constructing his characters from the outside in.

Acting became Olivier's lifeblood. He was singularly determined to become not a good actor but the greatest actor of his time, and he possessed the essential ingredients needed to become a star. He was charismatic and developed a larger than life presence that left many in awe. In 1930, Olivier married the actress Jill Esmond. Theirs was not a passionate relationship and Olivier later admitted that it had been a mistake. Still, Jill was pregnant with his son Tarquin when he and Vivien began their affair and his Victorian sense of duty to his wife and child prevented him from fully giving over to his lover. In the beginning of their relationship, Vivien played the role of pursuer. Tarquin was born in August 1936 and in October, shortly after *Fire Over England* wrapped, Vivien boldly followed Olivier and his wife to Capri. After that holiday, it was not long before Olivier's doubts about the future of their relationship were dispelled.

In the April 3, 1937 issue of *Picturegoer*, columnist Max Breen labeled Vivien "the most important recruit British films have ever had." He noted that "She is still not at all keen on going to Hollywood. She could go any day if she said the word. It's up to English studios to develop her over here." Korda developed Vivien in England, but not for the British screen. He was the foremost mogul in the British film industry and the only producer with solid enough connections to allow for his films to be distributed overseas. In 1933 he had secured a lucrative deal

with United Artists based on the success of *The Private Life of Henry VIII*, starring Charles Laughton.

Just as Korda's films had a crucial link to Hollywood and the world market, so too did the actors he had under contract. During the 1930s, the producer made no attempt to mold Vivien into a quintessentially British star. She was too glamorous and cosmopolitan to represent the middlebrow values that dominated British cinema at the time and so was cast as something else—the society girl who

comes to the assistance of her middle-class friends in *Look Up and Laugh* and *Storm in a Teacup*; a fashionable French spy working for German intelligence in *Dark Journey*; the vamp in MGM's first British production, *A Yank at Oxford*, which reunited her with her old friend Maureen O'Sullivan. In essence, Vivien was being groomed for a future in Hollywood.

In the spring of 1937, Vivien was again cast opposite Olivier in an adaptation of John Galsworthy's short story *The First and the Last*, scripted by Graham Greene. The film also reunited her with director Basil Dean, but this time her nervousness was replaced by indifference. Vivien plays Wanda, a young Russian girl whose lover, Larry Durant

Performing in the streets of St. Martin's Lane with Gentry (Tyrone Guthrie), Charles (Charles Laughton), and Constantine Dan (Larry Adler).

(Olivier) accidentally kills her long-absent husband. As financier, Korda took charge of casting the leads. Dean had directed his late lover, Meggie Albanesi, in a theatrical version of Galsworthy's story in the early 1920s. He wanted Clive Brook and Norwegian ballerina Vera Zorina in the film. When Brook declined, Korda cast Olivier and insisted that Vivien play the Albanesi role, much to Dean's skepticism.

Vivien and Olivier's reported behavior on the set showed none of the professionalism they would later be known for. Olivier made no secret of his aversion for film acting, particularly in his younger years, and some of his brashness rubbed off on Vivien. It only took a couple of days for Dean to realize that they were too preoccupied with their own emotions to concentrate on the work at hand. "Their joyous awareness of each other took the form of much laughter and giggling on the set," he wrote in 1973, referring to the pair as "two joyful miscreants." They, in turn, called Dean "Sugar." Makeup artist Stuart Freeborn had similar recollections. He was forced to ban Olivier from his room because as soon as he'd finished with Vivien's makeup, Olivier would "bustle in and kiss her until her face was a mess of powder and lipstick."

Korda appeared to have the same nonchalance about The First and the Last as his two stars did. In June, he shut down the set for a week to allow Vivien and Olivier to travel to Denmark for a special Old Vic production of Hamlet. Dean was infuriated and decided then to put an end to his directing career. As for the film itself, Korda shelved it for three years, only releasing it to cash in on the success of Gone With the Wind and Wuthering Heights. In 1940, Vivien and Olivier

went to see it at a cinema in New York, where it had been retitled 21 Days Together. They reportedly walked out halfway through.

The opportunity for Vivien to play Ophelia was likely a result of Olivier's influence at the Old Vic. She saw him perform as Hamlet no less than fourteen times during the 1937 season. Eager to develop her skills as a theatrical actress, Vivien was by now happily submitting herself to Olivier as a protégée. In their spare moments, he worked with her on her vocal range and offered practical advice. As the years went on, people accused Olivier as being "a mixture of Pygmalion and Svengali" where Vivien's career was concerned. However, he continually insisted that, "most of what she achieved was through her own ability and hard work." Tyrone Guthrie's company had been planning the special engagement since receiving an invitation from the Danish Tourist Association in May 1937. When original Ophelia Cherry Cottrell became unavailable, Vivien received a letter from Old Vic matriarch Lilian Baylis, inviting her to take over the role. For three weeks Vivien juggled a tiring schedule of filming in the morning and rehearsing in the evening.

Hamlet was to be staged in the courtyard of Kronborg Castle in Elsinore, in front of an audience of 2,500 but due to adverse weather on the opening night, the production was moved to the ballroom of the nearby Hotel Marienlyst. Although Guthrie had been scornful of Vivien's abilities during rehearsals and worried that her voice wouldn't be audible enough, Vivien surprised audiences and critics alike. An account written by a Danish theatergoer on June 8, 1937 describes Vivien's performance:

"Vivien L. who played Ophelia for the first time did not seem disturbed by the lack of support from a properly arranged stage, and she and Hamlet appeared and disappeared on the stage from various sides, reached by dashing along verandahs and cloak rooms along outside in the pouring rain.

"The papers say they have never seen a more crazy and charming Ophelia in the mad scene. (She played all evening with bare legs and ballet shoes.)"

Returning from Elsinore, Vivien and Olivier came clean to their spouses about their affair. According to Olivier's diary, Vivien left home just after midnight on June 16. Together they moved in to Durham Cottage in Chelsea, which would serve as their London base for nearly twenty years. The refusal of Holman and Esmond to grant divorces prolonged the disruption of both households for another three years. On Holman's part, he wanted Vivien to be completely sure of her decision before he went forward with legal proceedings. An actor's life was financially and emotionally uncertain, and Olivier was not yet the preeminent idol he was destined to become in later years. But it was a risk Vivien was willing to take. Leigh Holman would remain an amiable and steadfast presence throughout her life, often lending support in times of trouble. Gertrude Hartley became a surrogate mother to Suzanne, providing her with the stability she wouldn't have found growing up in Vivien's care.

The year 1938 was busy for Vivien. She played the title character in *Serena Blandish* at the Gate Theatre, and Tyrone Guthrie seemed to have a change of heart about her promise as an actress, casting her in his Christmas production of *A Midsummer Night's Dream* at the Old Vic. But her most important opportunity came when Korda loaned her out for *St. Martin's Lane* (called *Sidewalks of London* in America), produced by Erich Pommer for Mayflower Pictures and directed by Tim Whelan.

Vivien's character, Libby, was the closest thing that she was offered to a true star part during the interwar years. Libby is a Cockney waif; a singer and dancer who gets picked up by Charles Staggers (Charles Laughton) and his busking troupe before being discovered by a rich songwriter named Harley Prentiss (Rex Harrison) and made the star of a West End revue. Libby is also a professional pickpocket who does anything she can—including using other people—to get to the top of the professional ladder. Actor and author Simon Callow thoughtfully compared Vivien's interpretation of Libby to Louise Brooks's Lulu in the famous G. W. Pabst film *Die Büchse der Pandora* (*Pandora's Box*): ". . . She contains within her the spirit of anarchy, a real danger and unpredictability, that is almost Lulu-like: a daemon, a siren, a pussycat with the sharpest claws and a tongue that spits like a lynx." Indeed, the film has several elements of German Expressionism owing to Pommer's influence. It is most visible in the scene where Libby dances alone in an abandoned house, stark light and shadows lending an otherworldly quality to her fantasy.

St. Martin's Lane was the second film that paired Vivien with Rex Harrison (the first was in 1937's *Storm and a Teacup*, directed by Victor Saville). Although they "never so much as held hands," Harrison admitted to being in love with his leading lady, a situation that didn't go unnoticed by Olivier. As if guarding his territory, Olivier would show up to the set on days when Vivien was scheduled to do scenes with Harrison. According to Larry Adler, who played busker Constantine Dan, Olivier and Vivien would "disappear into her dressing-room and it was quite a business to get her back to work." Vivien enjoyed working with American director Tim Whelan, but she never warmed up to Charles Laughton, who had "expelled his own wife Elsa Lanchester from the cast when Korda offered to finance" the film.

Laughton was meant to be the star, but Vivien stole the show. Slipshod Cockney accent aside, her Libby is beautiful, vigorous, determined, and incandescent—qualities that would serve Vivien well on screen in the coming years. Her performance also foreshadows bigger things to come. Libby has ambitions of becoming famous on a global scale, summoning Hollywood with her references to Garbo. By the end of 1938, Vivien would embark on her own journey to international stardom.

Vivien as Titania and Robert Helpmann as Oberon in Tyrone Guthrie's production of *A Midsummer Night's Dream* at the Old Vic, 1937.

CHAPTER 2

SCARLETT

"Scarlett was a fascinating person, no matter what she did. But she was never a great person . . . In many ways, she wasn't a very admirable person. But one thing about her was admirable—her courage. She had more than I'll ever have."

—Vivien Leigh in *Movie Mirror*, 1940

David O. Selznick's highly publicized search for the perfect girl to star in *Gone With the Wind* was legendary even in its time. In the years leading up to the Second World War, an entire nation was under the spell of Margaret Mitchell's epic tale of love, loss, and survival during the American Civil War and Reconstruction. After its publication in May 1936, the book spread like wildfire, garnering both popular and critical praise, and winning the 1937 Pulitzer Prize for fiction. By 1939, there was hardly a soul in the U.S. and beyond who wasn't familiar with the infamous Scarlett O'Hara.

The list of famous names vying for the most sought-after role in film history read like a veritable who's who of Hollywood. Joan Crawford, Bette Davis, Katharine Hepburn, Lana Turner, Tallulah Bankhead, Paulette Goddard, Miriam Hopkins, and Joan Bennett had all at one point been mentioned to play the tempestuous southern belle. Selznick also sent scouts to the American South in search of "a girl who was not identified in the minds of the public with other roles, and who was a physical counterpart of the original Scarlett," with no suitable results. The film was backed by MGM mogul Louis B. Mayer (Selznick's

Vivien asked Angus McBean to photograph her in her best Scarlett O'Hara fashion and sent the photos to David O. Selznick, 1938.

father-in-law), and financier John Hay "Jock" Whitney. With a budget of nearly $4 million, it was the most expensive film produced to that date and the stakes were extremely high. When it came to casting the leads, Selznick had no room for error. "The public wanted [Clark] Gable to play Rhett; they were torn about Scarlett," recalled Evelyn Keyes, who played Scarlett's younger sister Suellen. Gable had his reservations about playing the roguish Rhett Butler. He didn't want the part, believing he could never live up to the public's expectations of how Rhett was supposed to act and look. Any discrepancy from the novel, and the fans would know it, he said. *Gone With the Wind* was a film that had the potential to either make or break a career and as the biggest male star at MGM, it was a risk he was reluctant to take. Eventually Gable gave in, but only after Selznick bribed him with a $50,000 bonus so that he could divorce his current wife, Rhea Langham, and marry the screwball comedienne Carole

Lombard. On August 24, 1938, Selznick secured his Rhett on a loan from Mayer. But Scarlett remained elusive until the night of December 10, 1938, when fortune brought Selznick face to face with Vivien Leigh.

"Everyone said I was mad to try for *Gone With the Wind*, but I wanted it and I knew I'd get it," Vivien said in 1960. The book had been published in England in 1937, and Vivien, like so many young women, took it to heart and immediately set her sights on Hollywood. While appearing in the flop play *Because We Must* at Wyndhams in the Charing Cross Road, Vivien gave everyone in the cast a copy of Mitchell's novel as an opening night present and urged them to read it. C. A. Lejeune, then film critic for *The Observer*, vividly remembered a river trip to Southend aboard the Golden Eagle with Vivien and Laurence Olivier while on assignment to write a behind-the-scenes story about the filming of *The First and the Last*:

LEFT: Vivien, pictured with Leslie Howard and Olivia de Havilland, looks over the script of *Gone With the Wind*.

RIGHT: Vivien presents producer David O. Selznick with daffodils during retakes for the beginning of the film.

25/1500 Elisabeth

"The conversation came round to *Gone With the Wind*, which was the fashionable book of the time and Hollywood's current casting problem. In a lighthearted way, Olivier remarked that he had been thinking of putting in for the part of Rhett Butler. I can see Vivien now, rising to her feet, all of five feet two or whatever it may be of her, quivering with excitement. She was certain of herself, and in that moment she was glorious. 'Larry,' she said, with the rain whipping against her face, 'you couldn't play Rhett, but I'm going to play Scarlett O'Hara.' He laughed at her; I laughed at her; everyone within hearing laughed at her. But she went to Hollywood and played Scarlett just the same."

Three of Walter Plunkett's costume designs for Scarlett O'Hara in *Gone With the Wind*.

TOP: Diane Fisher, the youngest extra in *Gone With the Wind*, asks the star for her autograph.

ABOVE: Behind the scenes on *Gone With the Wind* (1939).

LEFT: Vivien waits for her call during the filming of the famous crane shot at the Atlanta train depot.

RIGHT: Waiting to film the scene where Scarlett visits Rhett in jail.

Despite the odds stacked against her, Vivien refused to be discouraged. She knew that the only people she needed to convince of her rightness for Scarlett were Selznick and then-director George Cukor. Coincidentally, Cukor had seen Vivien in *Fire Over England* when it was released in the US, but was unimpressed. Very much aware of the power of her beauty, Vivien hired her friend and noted theater photographer Angus McBean to take a series of seductive headshots framing her in her best Scarlett fashion with the intention of mailing the photographs to Selznick. Now all she needed was a justifiable reason to travel to Califor-

nia and make her presence known.

Vivien's window of opportunity presented itself in the form of rising young director William Wyler. Fresh from guiding Bette Davis to her second Academy Award as Julie Marsden in *Jezebel*—Warner Bros.'s answer to *Gone With the Wind*—Wyler had come to London in search of a leading player to act in Samuel Goldwyn's adaptation of *Wuthering Heights*. The object of his fascination was not Vivien but Olivier, who he hoped to secure as Emily Brontë's dark and brooding anti-hero Heathcliff. It was a magnificent part, and Olivier would be mad to turn it down. But the actor was not easily convinced. A failed attempt at film stardom in the early 1930s that included being sacked by Greta Garbo from Rouben Mamoulian's 1933 film *Queen Christina* left Olivier with wounded pride and a bitter dislike for the film capital. He was also reluctant to leave Vivien behind at the height of their love affair. The only condition under which he'd accept the part, he told Wyler, was if Vivien starred opposite him as Cathy Earnshaw. It was an impossible request. Cathy had already been reserved as a star vehicle for Merle Oberon. Wyler instead offered Vivien the supporting role of Isabella Linton, to which she replied, "I'll play Cathy or I'll play nothing." The exchange was one Wyler remembered with great humor into old age: "I said to her, 'Look, Vivien. You're not yet known in America. Maybe someday you'll be a big star, but you're not yet known, and for a first part, you'll *never* get anything better than Isabella.' I made this deathless prediction. She sure showed me." Vivien saw that, despite his grudge, Olivier liked Wyler and the part of Heathcliff. With characteristic intuition and more than a touch of manipulation,

she was able to persuade him to change his mind. He sailed from Southampton on November 5, 1938, Vivien's twenty-fifth birthday, and within a month she was on her way to join him.

It was Olivier who unwittingly provided the crucial link between Vivien and her ambition. On the evening of December 10, Olivier took her to see his agent, Myron Selznick. Exactly what happened next has become so intricately woven into the fabric of Hollywood lore as to make it near impossible to separate fact from fiction, but Myron was convinced enough by Vivien's look to personally drive the couple to the Selznick International backlot in Culver City, where preliminary shooting had already begun on *Gone With the Wind*. There, as what had formerly been the set of RKO Pictures's *King Kong* went up in flames for the epic "Burning of Atlanta" scene, David O. Selznick finally met his Scarlett. It was an encounter he continuously propagated throughout his life, claiming that he never

ABOVE: Vivien and Gable burned up the screen as Scarlett O'Hara and Rhett Butler. In 2003, VH1 named them among the two hundred greatest American pop-culture icons.

A rumor has circulated that Vivien didn't like kissing Gable because he had bad breath. However, Vivien's end-of-life partner, Jack Merivale, recalled in 1978 that Vivien always spoke warmly of her *Gone With the Wind* costar.

RIGHT: Vivien and Clark Gable in a Clarence Sinclair Bull publicity shot.

recovered from that first look. Selznick's wife Irene maintained that the story was true, although no physical indicators of a planned meeting between the actress and producer have ever surfaced. To this day it remains unclear just how serendipitous the occasion actually was.

Margaret Mitchell was also won over by Vivien's appearance. "Naturally, I'm the only person in the world who knows what Scarlett really looks like but this girl looks charming," she wrote in a letter to

This stunning publicity shot of Vivien features the dress Scarlett wears on her New Orleans honeymoon with Rhett.

TOP: Despite difficulties with filming, Vivien and Gable had an amiable relationship while making the film.

ABOVE: Photograph by Clarence Sinclair Bull.

Selznick. "She has the most Irish look I have ever seen with the word 'Devil' in her eye." However, opposite Douglas Montgomery and Leslie Howard in the Cukor-directed screen tests it's clear that Vivien had more than just a physical resemblance to Mitchell's heroine. Unlike the other actresses whose tests have survived to this day, she proved that she wouldn't just act Scarlett; she would *become* Scarlett.

At Cukor's annual Christmas Day party in 1938, the director pulled Vivien aside and revealed that out of over 1,000 hopefuls, they were stuck with her. Previous commitments, including plans to appear as the Princess in Michael Powell and Tim Whelan's Technicolor fantasy *The Thief of Bagdad*, were broken in order to accept the role. In addition, she was forced to sign a standard contract that required her to make two pictures for Selznick and one for Korda every year until 1946. Her fee for six months of work on *Gone With the Wind* would be $25,000—a mere fraction of what Clark Gable was paid. Olivier accused the producer of exploitation, and was in turn reproached for selfishly trying to prevent Vivien from accepting the part. Selznick admonished that winning the role of a lifetime was compensation enough and that he'd be a fool to pay an unknown actress a star's salary. The conditions of the contract were less than ideal. She and Olivier worried about what her acceptance might mean for their relationship, as Olivier wasn't planning to stay in Hollywood for the long run. In the end, Vivien's determination outweighed her hesitancy. "Long contracts are stultifying. I only signed that one because I had to, to get Scarlett," she admitted in 1949. She had come too far to let the opportunity slip through her fingers and so she

plunged ahead, adopting Scarlett's attitude of dealing with consequences later.

The news that a British girl had been chosen to play such a quintessential American character set the Hollywood gossip colony abuzz with indignation. *Los Angeles Times* columnist Hedda Hopper called the decision "ludicrous" and summed up her own feelings through a letter sent in by angry reader Kay Clement Peddell, which better reflected American right-wing isolationist attitudes than it did general feelings about film culture: "One can hardly believe that a producer who intends to pour

Publicity shot relating to the last scene in the film, when Scarlett returns to Tara.

millions into a picture could possibly make such a colossal mistake. . . . Miss Leigh has lived and breathed England all her acting life. To trust her with the important role of an American woman of the Civil War period seems idiotic and almost an insult to American actresses and audiences." Both women predicted moviegoers would stay far away in protest.

Selznick anticipated the wave of backlash.

Together with publicity chief Russell Birdwell, he immediately set to work transforming his "discovery" from little-known British player to major Hollywood star. The process wasn't new to Vivien. She had undergone a similar routine when she signed with Korda in 1935. The goal was to solidify her in the public imagination as the ideal image of Scarlett. "In her physical characteristics as well as her ancestry, Miss Leigh resembles the heroine of Miss Mitchell's book," reads the official Selznick International press release. "She is five feet three, weighs 103 pounds, has green eyes, brown hair with a touch of red, and even possesses Scarlett's pointed chin." Eager film lovers who consumed the studio-controlled fan magazines learned that Vivien's parents were French and Irish, just as Scarlett's were. That the details may have been exaggerated or even fabricated made no difference. Manipulation was the driving force behind the star system and as far as public perception was concerned, Vivien was becoming an expert at playing the game.

It was only a matter of weeks before Vivien's enthusiasm for working on *Gone With the Wind* began to wane. In London, her affair with Olivier was common knowledge and Korda had nurtured their relationship from the beginning, using their romance for his own gains in *Fire Over England* and *21 Days Together*. But Hollywood was a different story. Selznick was unwilling to risk any word of publicity that might negatively affect his film. Fearing a scandal should word of their prospective divorces leak to the public, he forbade the lovers to live together. Not content to wait around

between film projects, Olivier traveled to New York in March 1939 to star opposite Katharine Cornell in *No Time for Comedy* on Broadway. Arriving on the east coast, Olivier wrote to Vivien's mother. The decision to work apart had been difficult, he said, but he believed it was the right one to make.

Tales of chaos escaped the closed set of *Gone With the Wind* throughout the spring of 1939. A completed script was never produced and scenes were shot out of order on a moment's notice with no seeming regard for continuity. "It is difficult, really," Vivien confided to journalist Paul Harrison in June. "It's especially trying, coming here day after day and not knowing what I'm to do or what mood I'm to assume without any rehearsals." Selznick, a notorious amphetamine addict, relied on a steady diet of cigarettes and Benzedrine to keep him going for days on end. He inserted himself into every aspect of production and became frustrated with what he was seeing in the daily rushes. Gable's costumes were too inadequate for

Vivien had a difficult time working with Victor Fleming, the tough-talking director who took over for George Cukor.

a star of his magnitude and building Tara plantation in the hills of Southern California was a poor substitute for shooting on location in Georgia. The film fell more behind schedule each passing day and was already over budget.

Vivien's only buffer against the mounting chaos was her affinity for George Cukor. Known in the business as a "woman's director" (he was gay and had an excellent rapport with many of his actresses), Cukor took special care in cultivating the performances of Vivien and Olivia de Havilland. Already feeling out of his element, Gable became disconcerted by the perceived lack of directorial attention being paid to his own performance by Cukor. "Playing Rhett Butler was an enormous responsibility for Clark and I can quite understand his qualms," recalls Olivia de Havilland more than seventy years later. "On the other hand, Vivien was born to play Scarlett, whom she perfectly understood entirely. I doubt that she ever for a single moment experienced Clark's uncertainty."

Selznick's personal assistant, Marcella Rabwin, recalled the uneasy dynamic between Vivien and

TOP: Vivien and her live-in Hollywood secretary, Sunny Lash, in 1939. Sunny adored both Vivien and Laurence Olivier, and worked for both of them when the couple returned to Hollywood in 1950 to film *A Streetcar Named Desire* and *Carrie*, respectively.

MIDDLE: Vivien signs braille copies of Margaret Mitchell's *Gone With the Wind*, 1939.

BOTTOM: Author Margaret Mitchell shares a laugh with Clark Gable and Vivien in Atlanta during the *Gone With the Wind* premiere.

Walter Plunkett designed this gown for Vivien to wear during the Atlanta premiere of *Gone With the Wind* in December 1939.

Gable during the first weeks of shooting: "Gable was always fighting for his life against this spirited girl. He felt that it was a woman's picture—that it was Scarlett O'Hara's picture. He said, 'I'm a big star! I don't want to be playing second fiddle to some dame.'" Selznick, too, had begun to view Cukor as a disadvantage to the film. He was brilliant at directing intimate moments, but Selznick thought he "lacked the big feel, the scope, the breadth of the production." After three weeks of filming, Cukor was let go and replaced by Victor Fleming, a tough-talking, macho director who had been working on *The Wizard of Oz* at MGM and happened to be one of Gable's best friends. The tables had suddenly turned and Vivien was deeply upset by the change, writing to Leigh Holman back in London that Cukor had been her "last hope of ever enjoying the picture."

The relationship between Vivien and her new director was strenuous from the beginning. Fleming, best known for helming action flicks and racy pre-code films like *Test Pilot* and *Red Dust*, both starring Clark Gable, lacked Cukor's sensitivity. He wanted his Scarlett to be a stereotypical spoiled bitch and was determined to goad it out of Vivien. "Ham it up," he would tell her whenever she sought advice on how to explore her character. Yet Vivien knew how important it was to convey Scarlett's sympathetic traits. Her costar may have been the most popular actor in Hollywood, but ultimately the film's success depended upon her ability to hold an audience for nearly four hours. She carried Mitchell's book around for reference and continuity purposes and, unbeknownst to Fleming, received secret coaching from Cukor on her Sundays off. "One day she arrived, took a swim, lay

down on a sofa and fell into a deep, absolute sleep," Cukor recalled in an interview with Gavin Lambert. "She was out for several hours, then she woke up, giggled, and told me, 'I was an absolute bitch on the set yesterday.' They'd been trying that very scene with Ashley, and she felt it wasn't right, so she made poor Victor Fleming trot over and screen the test. That was so typically straight-shooting of her, as an actress and as a human being." The arguments between actress and director often led to Fleming storming off the set in indignation. At one point, he allegedly told Vivien to "stick that script up her royal British ass" before threatening to drive his car off a cliff. Vivien was defiant and resolutely stood her ground. Her tenacity found its way into the film. As Selznick biographer David Thomson would write, the tension between Vivien and Fleming resulted in Vivien's Scarlett becoming "embittered, tougher, bitchier, and more dangerous—all to the benefit of the performance and never killing the tender wanton George had cultivated in her."

With Olivier away, Vivien focused on finishing the job as quickly as possible, often working inhuman hours and constantly pushing herself to the brink. She kept her composure on set, although the strain became visible to other cast members. Olivia de Havilland still recalls Vivien's resilience: "Vivien was very professional. Impeccably prepared. She always knew her lines and was always on time. She worked longer hours than anyone else in the cast, shooting sometimes after dinner so as to shorten the schedule and thus be able to rejoin Larry in New York. . . . The work week was from Monday to Saturday in those days. On returning to the studio after a four-week interval, I visited the stage where the company was just finishing work and barely recognized Vivien when she passed me on the way to her dressing room, as she had lost so much weight and seemed so depleted, physically and emotionally."

Sunny Lash, the studio-appointed secretary who lived with Vivien during the filming of *Gone With the Wind*, witnessed firsthand her struggle to deal with the situation. "Poor little Vivien, with her heart in New York and trying to put her mind on this—it's been awful," she wrote to Olivier on June 8. "Several times I thought she really was going mad. She warned me once that someday she would and I was beginning to believe her. . . . Working night and day and she never complains—

she'd kill herself to get through with this damn picture." The only thing that seemed to elevate her mood were the daily gifts, letters, and phone calls from Olivier.

On April 17, Vivien told Selznick she was pregnant but reported a false alarm after the producer arranged for an abortion. A few weeks later, Olivier informed her that he was considering staying on for an extended run of *No Time for Comedy*. Distraught and exhausted, Vivien took an

---

Laurence Olivier had to pretend he was in Atlanta to promote his upcoming film *Rebecca* (1940). After the film premiered, he and Vivien gave the press something to talk about by publicly announcing their engagement.

overdose of sleeping pills that same night. After receiving an anxious early-morning phone call from Sunny, Olivier frantically intervened from across the country. Sunny reassured him that it had been accidental, that Vivien hadn't realized the pills were so strong, but Olivier was convinced that she had done on it purpose in an act of defiance and recklessness. He wrote a long and passionate letter to Vivien ending with, "I'm afraid you lead your loving ones one hell of a dance and that's *terribly* naughty . . . don't give way in front of the common herd like this." Recognizing the underlying source of Vivien's distress, Selznick arranged for her to spend a weekend with Olivier in Kansas City. It provided only a short respite from her grueling workload but it was enough to ignite a flame that

carried her through to the end of shooting. Each night after returning home from the studio, she took a pen to her calendar and with an exclamation of "whoopee!" crossed off another day.

After filming her last scene on June 27, Vivien boarded a plane for New York, where Olivier was wrapping up his current engagement. She had no desire to continue living in Scarlett's skin. "All I'm conscious of is a blessed relief," she told *Movie Mirror*. "I'm beginning to feel sane again—almost normal. For five months, except for five days and Sundays off, I had to work at being Scarlett from nine in the morning until nine at night. Then, when I would fall into bed exhausted, I couldn't sleep. Every nerve in my body was pounding. The last month or so, I had to take tonics to keep going. At

LEFT: Vivien and Olivier with Olivia de Havilland and financier Jock Whitney during the Los Angeles premiere of *Gone With the Wind*, December 28, 1939.

RIGHT: Olivia de Havilland, Laurence Olivier, Vivien, and David O. Selznick at the Café Trocadero in West Hollywood after the Los Angeles premiere of *Gone With the Wind*.

the end, I was quite raving mad—ready for a lunatic asylum. . . . I still wonder when I'll have caught up on my sleep." Her involvement with *Gone With the Wind* was far from over but she wasted little time in focusing her energies on what she hoped would be her next starring role.

Continuing with the trend of adapting classic novels for the screen, Selznick chose Daphne du Maurier's gothic mystery *Rebecca* as his follow-up to *Gone With the Wind*. He had recruited Alfred Hitchcock from Britain that same year and assigned the budding auteur to direct the story of a young woman who marries the handsome and troubled owner of a Cornish estate, only to learn that the specter of his dead wife is still very much alive.

Vivien showed little interest in the film initially, but jumped at the opportunity to work opposite Olivier when he was cast as the mysterious Maxim de Winter. "Vivien was determined to play opposite Larry," Irene Mayer Selznick wrote in her autobiography. "This was a woman obsessively in love. All of the qualities which made her the perfect choice for Scarlett made her the worst possible one for this role." She was allowed to make two screen tests and Olivier half-heartedly lobbied on her behalf, but later admitted that he didn't think her right for the part. Everyone, including Hitchcock, agreed. Vivien's personality was deemed too strong to convincingly portray a timid, unattractive, and nameless character. Looking back on the film,

Hitchcock revealed in an interview with former Cinémathèque Française director Henri Langlois that he thought Vivien had been much better suited to play the omnipresent title character, Rebecca: "Vivien Leigh was absolutely right to play Rebecca, but Rebecca never appears in the film, so neither does Vivien. And for people who knew about the real life affair between Olivier and Leigh, that would have intruded on any illusion."

Returning with Olivier and her mother from a holiday in Europe aboard the *Île de France* in the summer of 1939, Vivien received a disappointing telegram from Selznick. She would make her next film on loan to MGM. The part of Mrs. de Winter had been given to Joan Fontaine.

The premiere of *Gone With the Wind* was not an occasion that Vivien particularly looked forward to. In fact, she dreaded it, telling reporter Roger Carroll, "I'd like to be a million miles away, and not have to wonder how much of the applause is inspired by the picture, and how much is generated by the glamour of the event and the presence of the stars." She was acutely aware that the success of the film largely rested on her shoulders. Such a responsibility would have been a burden for any established star to carry, let alone someone who had yet to claim that title. Vivien's anxiety was compounded by Selznick's hesitation to let Olivier accompany her to the celebration. By this time the press had caught on that she and Olivier were an off-screen item, but Selznick was still cautious about letting them be seen in public together until after his film was safely on its way to box-office gold. When Vivien flatly refused to go alone, the producer was left with no choice but to relent.

Two weeks before Christmas, the cast mem-bers—excluding Leslie Howard, who had returned to England for war service, and Hattie McDaniel, who fell victim to the segregation laws still in effect in the American South—arrived in Georgia for the biggest film event of the decade. For all of her nervousness and misgivings, Vivien appeared every inch the star from the moment she stepped off the plane alongside Olivia de Havilland and Selznick at Candler Field in Atlanta. Newsreel footage captured a glamorous and composed young woman as she waved to the press and shook hands with Mayor William B. Hartsfield. Always in the background but present nonetheless was Olivier, in town under the guise of promoting the upcoming release of *Rebecca*.

Three years after beginning its journey from page to screen, *Gone With the Wind* premiered "in a blaze of lights and glory" on December 15, 1939. According to *TIME* magazine, 300,000 people lined Atlanta's famous Peachtree Street and "crowds larger than the combined armies that fought in Atlanta in 1864 waved Confederate flags, tossed confetti till it seemed to be snowing, gave three different versions of the Rebel yell, whistled, cheered, goggled" as the star-studded motorcade made its way to Loew's Grand Theater. Before taking their seats inside, the major players were asked to address the crowd and give a short speech for the radio. Mitchell thanked the American public for being so kind to her and her "poor Scarlett." Gable asked that the fans keep their distance so

Vivien became the first British woman to win an Oscar in the Best Actress category for her iconic performance as Scarlett O'Hara.

that he could view the film as a spectator rather than a star. And Vivien, recalling her own emotional journey from London to Los Angeles and the six challenging months spent living and breathing Scarlett, tearfully expressed her gratitude for Southern hospitality: "Ladies and gentlemen, I've spent a good deal of time on Peachtree Street this year, and now that I'm here it feels just as if I were coming home. And the warmth and kindness of your wonderful welcome has made it the happiest homecoming I could possibly imagine. I greet you and I want to thank you with all my heart."

The thunderous ovation that reverberated throughout the theater that December night in Atlanta was enough to tell Vivien that she had exceeded the public's expectations. Critics, too, were unanimous in their praise. "Miss Leigh's Scarlett has vindicated the absurd talent quest that indirectly turned her up," wrote Frank Nugent in *The New York Times*. "She is so perfectly designed for the part by art and nature that any other actress in the role would be inconceivable." Even Hedda Hopper, who had so vehemently opposed Vivien winning the role, was forced to eat her own words. "Now, by golly, I've got to congratulate [Selznick] and everyone concerned for picking Vivien Leigh. It is an incredible, unbelievable performance. . . . In fact, she didn't play Scarlett—she was Scarlett. Hers wasn't a performance, it was a whole career."

Vivien's place on the A-list was firmly solidified on February 29, 1940, when the film colony's elite descended upon the Ambassador Hotel on Wilshire Blvd to celebrate the twelfth annual Academy Awards. It was a night of many firsts in Hollywood history. *Gone With the Wind* swept the show with a then-unprecedented ten awards, including

Best Picture, Director, Screenplay, and Color Cinematography. Hattie McDaniel became the first African American to win an Oscar, for her moving performance as Scarlett's stalwart Mammy. Vivien arrived wearing an unconventional floral print gown by leading female designer Irene Gibbons and an air of self-assurance that was entirely her own. She was considered the front-runner, and her victory hardly came as a surprise. Having been tipped off earlier that evening, the *Los Angeles Times* jumped the gun and published the list of winners meant for the next day's paper. Just as she had run off with the part of Scarlett, Vivien beat out the likes of Greta Garbo, Bette Davis, Irene Dunne, and Greer Garson to become the first British winner in the Best Actress category.

Acting in *Gone With the Wind* was later considered by Vivien to be one of the defining moments in her life. She had proved she could act well when the part allowed her room to flourish. The film also marked the first time in her career that her talent received as much acclaim as her beauty. With a single performance she achieved a level of cultural significance that would not be reached by any other British actress of her generation. And her embodiment of Scarlett O'Hara would take on more meaning than anyone at the time could have known. First in the United States and then in Britain and beyond, she became, through Scarlett, an international symbol of unwavering determination in the face of war, poverty, and suppression.

At the young age of twenty-six, Vivien Leigh found herself to be the most sought-after actress in Hollywood. Yet, as it had in 1935 after her opening night in *The Mask of Virtue*, her success proved a mixed blessing. The applause had barely died

A rare color photograph of the winners' table during the 1940 Academy Awards ceremony. Pictured from left to right: Irene Mayer Selznick, Jock Whitney, Olivia de Havilland, David O. Selznick, Vivien, and Laurence Olivier.

down before critics began wondering whether she would ever mange to escape Scarlett's shadow. "Will Vivien Leigh be Gone with the Wind?" was the question posed by Harriet Parsons in the *Los Angeles Examiner*. Overseas, Hubert Cole of *Picturegoer* wondered whether Vivien would always be "Little Miss Echo" and predicted that Scarlett might well kill her career if she didn't make a supreme effort to avoid typecasting.

On a personal level, Vivien's achievement was a source of jealousy for Olivier, who had learned to better appreciate film acting under Wyler's direction but did not yet possess Vivien's apparent naturalness in front of the camera. Still, Vivien firmly believed that Olivier was a born actor and that her own talent was the result of his teachings. From

1937 they had worked together to cultivate her skill in the hopes that one day they might become the West End's answer to revered Broadway couple Alfred Lunt and Lynn Fontanne. "After *Gone With the Wind*, Vivien was the 'hottest' thing in pictures; she was a really big movie star," said George Cukor. "In all this her professional attitude to Larry never changed in the slightest . . . their relative positions had not altered in any way; he was the great, talented actor, and she the promising, young, not too important actress who had not yet accomplished a great deal . . . she always felt that his was the great and important destiny, and she never let anything interfere with this. I think her incentive for her development as an actress was to be on par with him."

At the time, Olivier's definition of success made no allowances for film stardom. Cinema was a director's medium. Great acting, he believed, could only be achieved through direct interaction with a live audience, not pieced together in an editing room. If he and Vivien were serious about their careers, they couldn't spend too much time dallying on film sets. They needed to re-establish themselves on the legitimate stage as quickly as possible.

LEFT: Proud producer Selznick shares Vivien's Oscar glory after the ceremony at the Ambassador Hotel in Los Angeles, February 29, 1940.

RIGHT: After the ceremony, Vivien and Olivier were photographed together at their home in Beverly Hills. Vivien wore an unconventional gown by designer Irene Gibbons and a topaz pendant from Van Cleef & Arpels, a gift from Olivier.

CHAPTER 3

THE WAR YEARS

"I really feel that anyone who is British and in America, and can do something to help, should come back to England . . ."

—Vivien Leigh, 1941

Reflecting on his experience directing the 1940 version of *Waterloo Bridge*, Mervyn LeRoy fondly recalled how Vivien "always said it was the best thing she ever did." Robert E. Sherwood's semi-autobiographical play, about a soldier who falls in love with a chorus-girl-turned-prostitute in WWI London, originally appeared on the screen in 1931. Helmed by famed horror director James Whale, Universal Pictures's unflinching pre-code film had been critically praised for its deft handling

of controversial themes. The film rights were taken over by MGM in 1939 and Louis B. Mayer, eager to capitalize on the financial success of *Gone With the Wind*, decided it would be perfect for Vivien.

S. N. Behrman allegedly modified the screenplay with her and Olivier in mind for the leads and Vivien felt excited at the prospect of working with her now-fiancé after being denied the opportunity to star in *Rebecca*. But Mayer had other plans. When Olivier was cast as Darcy in *Pride and Prejudice*, Vivien tried to persuade the producer to let her play Elizabeth Bennett. Joan Crawford could star in *Waterloo Bridge*, she reasoned. Or Mayer

---

Publicity portrait for MGM.

MODERN SCREEN

JUNE
10
CENTS

THE LARGEST
CIRCULATION
OF ANY SCREEN
MAGAZINE

VIVIEN
LEIGH

**"DON'T CALL ME
A GREAT LOVER!"**
INSISTS
LAURENCE OLIVIER

could find another British actor for Darcy, thereby freeing Olivier to play Roy Cronin opposite her Myra Lester. Instead, Greer Garson signed on to *Pride and Prejudice* and Vivien was reunited with her *A Yank at Oxford* costar Robert Taylor. This "classic piece of miscasting" fed into a growing feeling of resentment at the lack of control she had over her career. "I'm afraid it will be a dreary job," she wrote to Leigh Holman. "As I have no jurisdiction whatsoever as to what happens to me, or what I'm given to do, I'll just have to like it."

LEFT: After *Gone With the Wind*, Vivien became the most sought-after actress in Hollywood.

BELOW: Vivien, director Mervyn LeRoy, and Robert Taylor chat on the first day of filming *Waterloo Bridge* at MGM (1940).

Once filming started, however, Vivien found the work more enjoyable than she had anticipated. LeRoy was a breath of fresh air compared to Victor Fleming. They shared a mutual camaraderie born out of respect for one another's intellect and fast-paced work ethic. Even more than her fondness for LeRoy was her appreciation for W. S. Van Dyke, who temporarily stepped behind the camera early on during shooting and was capable of getting "a day's work done before most directors can even work themselves into the creative mood." She also got along well with Taylor, who praised her for enhancing his own performance.

Over the years, *Waterloo Bridge* has been largely written off by biographers as a footnote in Vivien's career; a popular and interesting film in its day but hardly a role fit to follow Scarlett. Yet for Vivien, who firmly believed that the only way to

"I knew I had to find you again... quickly!"

truly grow as an artist was to play as many different roles as possible, it provided an opportunity to stretch her acting abilities beyond the mold set in place by *Gone With the Wind*. Myra glides through the chiaroscuro London streets like a sylph. In the film's most climactic scene, she prowls Waterloo Station, greeting soldiers freshly home from the front. Suddenly the camera closes in on her face as she recognizes Roy, whom she thought had been killed in action. The subtle shifts in Vivien's expression are as heartbreakingly effective as if she had been acting for the silent screen. It emerges today as one of her most poignant performances.

When not in front of the camera, Vivien spent

Today, *Waterloo Bridge* remains one of Vivien's most beloved films.

most of her free time in her trailer with Olivier going over the script for *Romeo and Juliet*. Neville Chamberlain's declaration of war on September 9, 1939 threw any long-term plans for the future into disarray. There was no time to think about contractual obligations now. "Everything seems so useless these days, and so unimportant. Even acting is inconsequential when one thinks of what is going on over there," Vivien said in 1940. With war an ominous certainty, she and Olivier turned their eyes to England and began making plans to return home and offer themselves to whatever branch of service would take them. They had been advised by Olivier's friend Duff Cooper at the Ministry of Information in London that British actors in Hollywood would be of more help staying in California until further notice. When George Cukor suggested they stage *Romeo and Juliet* and take the production on tour across the country, the couple saw it as the perfect solution.

Selznick was reluctant to allow Vivien to participate, believing that appearing in a play so soon after *Gone With the Wind* would be bad for his investment. But the plan seemed foolproof. She and Olivier would have a chance to prove their cultural worth to film-centric America. At the same time, they were sure the dazzling aura of their film idol images would bring in a large sum of money. Not to mention the draw of their physical relationship, which had taken on a roseate hue in the eyes of the public since the announcement of their engagement following the premiere of *Gone With the Wind*. "Theirs was certainly a passionate relationship at the time," Olivia de Havilland remembers, "I think Vivien and Larry were almost obsessed with each other. Both of them had a great deal of charm and made an extraordinarily attractive couple under social circumstances."

Encouraged by the artistic opportunity in front of them, Olivier, who had played a virile Romeo at the Old Vic in 1935, designated himself actor, director, and producer. Riding a wave of optimism,

RIGHT & NEXT SPREAD: MGM photographer Laszlo Willinger took stunning publicity portraits of Vivien as ballerina Myra Lester. He considered Vivien to be one of his favorite subjects.

they invested $96,000 of their own money. Vivien
threw herself into the role with characteristic gusto.
She would, Olivier promised, make a devastating
Juliet. "Miss Leigh has youth with strength. Pathos
with comedy. And exceptional fire," he told *Modern Screen*. "She's going to surprise everyone."

The play opened to packed houses and mixed
reviews in San Francisco in May 1940, and it soon
became clear that the production wouldn't be able
to live up to expectations. Advanced bookings had
piled up nicely due, in part, to publicity promising
audiences that they would see real lovers making
love in public. Instead, they were treated to mal-
functioning sets and performances that suggested
little of the talent and commanding presence that
would later make the Oliviers the most popular
theatrical couple in Britain. "Last week one of the
most glittering first-night audiences in Manhattan's
history saw a production of *Romeo and Juliet* that
was not merely weak or spotty, but calamitous,"
wrote *TIME* magazine as the play gallantly trudged
into New York after a lukewarm reception in
Chicago. "The audience had been enthusiastic—
but hardly anyone came to see us at the end of the
last night," Vivien remembered. "Early in the morning we read the notices. And they were disastrous.
I had ordered cases of wine to be delivered to the
Hotel. Now I knew we couldn't afford to stay there.
So I went down and told the manager that we
would be leaving that day."

TOP: Vivien had known Robert Taylor since 1937 and
enjoyed working with him in *Waterloo Bridge*. He thought
her a good actress, and admitted that she helped better his
performance.

BOTTOM: Clark Gable visits Vivien on the set of *Waterloo
Bridge* at MGM.

MGM publicity portraits by Laszlo Willinger show Vivien in quintessential 1940s fashion.

Vivien fared best in the reviews but it was not the unanimous praise they had hoped for. In looks, she was perfect for Juliet. Her genuine effort to act the play as written was appreciated, but Broadway's seasoned columnists felt she lacked the experience to effectively convey the depth of Shakespeare's romantic prose. The crux of the play's failure was attributed to Olivier taking on more than he could handle. In the critics' minds they were "jumped up little movie stars seeking to go legit." As Radie Harris, former journalist and friend of Vivien's, later put it, "the production went down like a lead balloon" and the couple lost their entire combined savings.

Failure was a bitter pill to swallow. Broke and stranded in the US, the idea of returning to England began to seem more like a dream than a reality until the summer of 1940, when Vivien and Olivier received a cable from Alexander Korda. Rather than return to London, the fiercely patriotic producer chose to stay in Hollywood when war broke out in order to oversee the finishing touches on *The Thief of Bagdad*. In doing so, he was branded a traitor by the British film community. Not wanting to alienate himself further, Korda set out to direct a pro-British propaganda film to prove his loyalty to his adopted country. Keeping with his signature style of making epic historical dramas, he chose the famous love affair between sea captain

TOP: Vivien and Olivier study the script for *Romeo and Juliet* while on break from filming *Waterloo Bridge* and *Pride and Prejudice*, respectively.

BOTTOM: News of Vivien and Olivier's production of *Romeo and Juliet* made front pages overseas as well as in the U.S. *The Sketch* was one of England's most popular newspapers in the 1940s.

No. 2408—Vol. CXC.   WEDNESDAY, MAY 15, 1940.   ONE SHILLING.

VIVIEN LEIGH AND LAURENCE OLIVIER
PLAY ROMEO AND JULIET.

VIVIEN LEIGH, who has made such a big success as Scarlett O'Hara in the much-discussed film "Gone With the Wind," is playing Juliet to LAURENCE OLIVIER'S Romeo in the U.S.A. production of "Romeo and Juliet," due this month in New York. Her Shakespearean experience includes her appearance' as Ophelia in "Hamlet" with Laurence Olivier at Elsinore in 1937, with the Old Vic Company; and she was Titania in the Old Vic production of "A Midsummer Night's Dream" in the same year. Laurence Olivier has appeared in most of the famous Shakespearean rôles.

Horatio Lord Nelson and social-climbing Emma Hamilton as his subject and offered Vivien and Olivier the starring roles in what would be called *That Hamilton Woman*. Korda's generosity was something Vivien never forgot: "When I made *Lady Hamilton* for [Korda] in Hollywood during the war there wasn't very much money about and he gave me a bonus so I could send my mother and my daughter Suzanne, who was six years old, to Canada to get away from the bombing. There aren't many producers who would do that."

On August 30, 1940, shortly before filming began, Vivien and Olivier tied the knot in a secret midnight ceremony at the San Ysidro Ranch in picturesque Santa Barbara, California. They had been telling the press for some time that they would be married when their respective divorces came through, but the decision to elope happened so suddenly that it caught even Vivien off-guard. "I wired you as soon as it was done," Vivien wrote to Leigh Holman on September 4, adding that she "would have written beforehand if I had known myself it was going to take place as soon as that." The only people who were told in advance were their friends Ronald and Benita Colman, and publicist Russell Birdwell, who was instructed to hold off on a press release. Garson Kanin and Katharine Hepburn were summoned at the last possible

Preparing for a publicity shoot during rehearsals for *Romeo and Juliet*, May 1940.

Vivien and Olivier at a press conference for *Romeo and Juliet* in Chicago, 1940. The play was given a lukewarm reception in the Windy City.

minute to be best man and maid of honor. "I really didn't know Vivien or Larry that well," Hepburn told Alexander Walker. "But Gar Kanin and I sat in the back of Larry's Packard and Larry drove and, of course, Vivien sat close to him in the front seat. I remember feeling the conversation she and Larry were having as we drove along was, well, rather racy." Afterward, the Colmans offered their yacht, *Dragoon*, as a honeymoon vessel and the newlyweds set sail for Avalon Bay at Catalina Island.

Vivien and Olivier had spent so much effort making sure news of their marriage didn't leak to the public that the event became anticlimactic. The next day, as they lay on the deck of the boat enjoying the late summer weather, they kept their ears peeled for a public announcement. It turned out that Russell Birdwell was a little too good at keep-

ing secrets. When they finally heard the news reported on the radio later that evening, it came as a happy relief. The Oliviers's marriage legitimized them in the eyes of the public and formed the basis of a legend that would only grow in stature as the years went on.

That Hamilton Woman was the third and final film the couple starred in together, and is, in the words of historian Molly Haskell, the one that best "encapsulates the eternal yearning, theirs and ours, for a romantic illusion, the preferred 'truth' as created by art and given its most powerful popular form in classical Hollywood cinema." Different performance styles have been cited by at least one Vivien biographer as the reason behind the Oliviers's diverging screen careers. The real culprit, however, was the war. Korda attempted to kill two birds with one stone by appealing to different audience sensibilities in both Hollywood and Britain. Olivier's performance is more firmly rooted in the documentary realism movement that would largely define the British film industry in the 1940s. According to biographer Anthony Holden, Olivier had wanted to explore his character with more psychological insight, but he agreed that, given the underlying message of the film, it would be unwise to portray Nelson as anything other than the "cardboard hero required by the times." In contrast, Vivien was allowed to "give full reign to the mercurial temperament and star glamour" she had acquired in her two previous films. In René Hubert's

decorative period costumes and aided by the same visionary style of cinematography that made Rudolph Maté famous during his collaborations with Carl Theodor Dreyer in the late 1920s, Vivien lends vital life to what would otherwise have been a dry example of overt flag-waving.

At the end of the six-week shoot, the Oliviers wasted little time in saying their goodbyes to America. In December, they boarded the S.S. *Excambion* in New York and without so much as a backward glance, Vivien left behind what would surely have been a long and extremely lucrative

The ill-fated lovers in their ill-fated production.

Hollywood career for an uncertain future in war-torn England.

Arriving in London in the midst of an air raid, the couple immediately set out to find work. Olivier, who at thirty-three was too old for active duty, lent a patriotic voice to Michael Powell and Emeric Pressburger's *49th Parallel* and Humphrey Jennings's poetic short documentary *Words for Battle* before joining the Fleet Air Arm. For Vivien, gaining employment proved more difficult. She visited Tyrone Guthrie at his home near Manchester to inquire about the possibility of rejoining the Old Vic Company. Guthrie, who had been glad to have her in his cast in 1938 and who acted with her in *St. Martin's Lane*, was now skeptical of her Hollywood star image. "The audience would be there for the wrong reasons," he said. Adding insult to injury, he told her she was "not a good enough actress—not on the stage."

During the two years Vivien spent in Hollywood, her native industry had undergone shifts in both style and critical perspective. The patriotic films that now garnered praise from arbiters of quality cinema such as *The Observer*'s C. A. Lejeune and Dilys Powell of *The Sunday Times* were largely male-dominated. On the rare occasion that a female character took center stage, the roles were better suited to actresses like Celia Johnson or Wendy Hiller, who were relatable to female audiences, but who lacked Vivien's ethereal presence. However, despite the absence of suitable new roles, Vivien was still a competitive force on the British screen. *Gone With the Wind* had been released in England in April 1940 and ran at the Empire Leicester Square in central London for four consecutive years, effectively becoming the longest-running film of the war.

Vivien officially returned to the stage on March 14, 1942. Olivier made arrangements with Hugh "Binkie" Beaumont of H. M. Tennent management for her to appear in a revival of George Bernard Shaw's *The Doctor's Dilemma*. Jennifer Dubedat

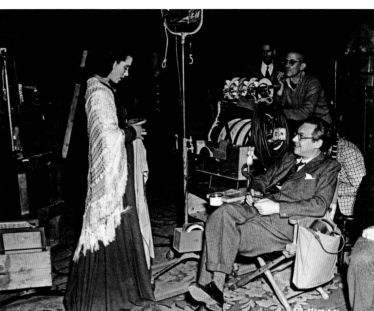

PREVIOUS PAGE LEFT: In their last film together, the Oliviers played real-life lovers Horatio Nelson and Emma, Lady Hamilton.

PREVIOUS PAGE RIGHT: While filming *That Hamilton Woman* for Alexander Korda, the Oliviers rented a house in Beverly Hills that came with a loveable sheep dog called Jupiter. "Jupee" occasionally came with them to the General Service Studios during filming.

TOP LEFT: As Horatio Nelson and Emma Hamilton in *That Hamilton Woman* (1941).

TOP RIGHT: Vivien had a life-long affinity for Alexander Korda, who gave her a bonus so she could send her mother and daughter Suzanne to Canada to escape the bombing in England.

RIGHT: Vivien is considered by some to have been at her most beautiful in *That Hamilton Woman* (1941).

TOP: Vivien was yachting at Catalina Island on the day Neville Chamberlain declared war on Germany. This photo, snapped by David Niven, shows Vivien and Olivier during

BOTTOM LEFT & RIGHT: The Oliviers eloped in a midnight ceremony at Ronald Colman's San Ysidro Ranch in Santa Barbara. They went to lengths to keep it a secret.

Picturegoer and Film Weekly. Registered at the G.P.O. as a newspaper

No. 466 (New Series), Vol. 9: April 27, 1940

Picturegoer

Incorporating **Film Weekly** 2ᵈ

Clark GABLE
& *Vivien* LEIGH

was "a terribly affected creature" and the part was more ornamental than meaningful. Vivien didn't find her role overly interesting, but she did think it good discipline.

Throughout the twelve-week provincial tour leading up to the London opening, she experienced firsthand the strange vitality of wartime life. Olivier was stationed near Winchester and she endured long journeys to spend weekends with him, with volumes of Dickens as her constant comfort on the cold, uncomfortable trains. She was "glad to be back among her own people, to be sharing with them the rough and the smooth." And the public admired that their "local girl [who] made very, very good" had left behind her dazzling film career for buzz bombs and blackouts.

Tyrone Guthrie's prediction that audiences would flock to see Scarlett on the stage turned out to be correct. *The Doctor's Dilemma* ran at the Theatre Royal Haymarket for over a year. National Gallery director Kenneth Clark often walked across the road to have tea with Vivien in her dressing room. "At first I went because I enjoyed looking at her," Clark said, likening her to a renaissance sculpture. "But very soon I went because I enjoyed her company and was fascinated by her character. She was not only intelligent; she had style . . . Vivien's conversation had much in common with that of Gwendoline in *The Importance of Being Earnest*."

Cecil Beaton was another figure from the art world that got to know Vivien better during the war. He had photographed her for *Vogue* several times since her sudden rise to fame in 1935 and found her good company when they met in Edinburgh during the play's pre-London run. They dined out after one performance and Vivien obliged fans with autographs. Afterward, they stayed up in the lobby of Vivien's hotel, talking until dawn. "Vivien is almost incredibly lovely," Beaton said, "Hollywood is at her feet. She knows if all else fails she has merely to go out there and make a fortune. . . . She is madly in love with her husband—who adores her—& is convinced he is a much greater person than herself. Her former husband dotes upon & adores her still—she is unspoiled—has many loyal friends & only ambition to improve as an actress." Vivien and Beaton remained on good terms until 1948, when they had a falling out over costumes for Olivier's production of *The School for Scandal*.

Despite the success of *The Doctor's Dilemma*, Vivien felt she could do more to help the war effort and suggested volunteering as an ambulance driver, an auxiliary policewoman, or doing fire watch duty on the roof of the theater. But Beaumont, who would go on to produce many of Vivien's plays in the coming years, convinced her that there was no greater contribution than "giving pleasure to the public, cheering up the servicemen on leave, and keeping people happy." In this she certainly excelled, and in May 1943, he gave her the opportunity to accompany a group of Old Vic players to entertain Allied troops that had fought in the Desert Campaign.

Rommel and the Afrika Korps had just been defeated when the Old Vic Spring Party arrived in Gibraltar for the first leg of their North African tour.

Although she did not appear in any British films during the war, Vivien was one of the most powerful forces on the British screen. *Gone With the Wind* ran at the Empire, Leicester Square, for four consecutive years.

Vivien was the only non-musical performer in the concert party but was undoubtedly the biggest draw. She recited "You Are Old, Father William" from *Alice's Adventures in Wonderland* and the patriotic "Plymouth Hoe" by Clemence Dane. This was topped off by a burlesque called "Scarlett O'Hara, the Terror of Tara," written by *New Statesman* satirist Sagittarius, which poked fun at her famous film performance.

Over the course of the next three months, the Spring Party traversed the African desert, performing under the scorching sun for thousands of entertainment-starved soldiers in Algeria, Tunisia, and Libya. Vivien wrote frequently to Olivier—in Ireland filming Shakespeare's *Henry V*—about her adventures and the challenges the company faced in staging pop-up shows in a battle-scarred region. It was an exhausting but wholly unique experience. On July 15 she reported from Tunis that she was sleeping in the bed recently vacated by Nazi general Hans-Jürgen von Arnim. Their stage manager had been left behind in Algeria on suspicion of espionage, "so you can imagine the difficulties during the show. . . . Most of the stage hands, etc are very pleasant, but there are still those who try to sabotage the proceedings. Nothing seems to matter though, because now we are really playing to the boys who deserve it & haven't seen anything except fighting for months."

From Tripoli she wrote of a private performance the company put on for King George VI. It was, she told Olivier, "one of the most exciting" moments of her life; her happiness diminished only by the fact that he was not there living the experience with her:

". . . I felt so thrilled & frightened & in ten minutes the show had started & there we were on a little wide shallow terrace with 3 wide steps in front of us with footlights, and 3 beautiful arches behind for our stage set. The audience was sitting v. near and we could just see their faces in the moonlight. And then silhouetted against the sea. We did a v. cut version, only 45 minutes or so I just did Father William *and* Plymouth. The beauty of the setting was quite breathtaking only a very light breeze. White marble and moonlight. And then at the end when we say King—it was just too much tears sprang from my eyes & I felt a complete ass as we stood attention until he'd moved away. I think everyone was in the same condition, though.

The Oliviers serve hot tea to British soldiers in London, 1941.

"In a very few minutes he came round and we were all presented. He said he liked Plymouth very much & asked me about it and also suggested that I should cut The White Cliffs (which he always carried with him) and make an act of it—he seemed to have enjoyed himself greatly & I thought he looked absolutely wonderful. We then all adjourned to a swimming pool & had a jolly ripping gin."

LEFT: Vivien participated in the war effort before leaving Hollywood, knitting balaclava helmets for soldiers as part of the Bundles for Britain charity. Here, in 1940, Olivier lends a helping hand.

RIGHT: Entertaining troops in North Africa as part of the Old Vic Spring Party, 1943.

Vivien returned to London in August and set up house with Olivier at Old Prestwick in Gerrards Cross, not far from London. She and Olivier had both been discouraged by their inability to secure permission from Selznick for her to play Princess Catherine in Olivier's *Henry V*. The film would go on to do remarkably well overseas due to the Rank Organization's method of road-show exhibition, wherein the film was released in art house cinemas in select cities, allowing the profits to trickle in slowly. However, Selznick, who still had Vivien under contract, believed the part to be too small for a star of her magnitude. If British producers wanted to utilize Hollywood's hottest property, they had to come up with a film suitable enough in size and content to compare to *Gone With the*

Vivien returned to the stage in 1942 as Jennifer Dubedat in George Bernard Shaw's *The Doctor's Dilemma*. Photo by Angus McBean.

Wind. In the three years that Vivien had been back in England, director Gabriel Pascal's adaptation of George Bernard Shaw's *Caesar and Cleopatra* was the first film to meet Selznick's criteria. Shaw's screenplay provided the prestige angle and with J. Arthur Rank's financial backing, it would be the most expensive British film produced to that date.

Shaw's kittenish queen greatly appealed to Vivien's theatrical sensibilities, and it was a role she was confident she could excel in. Rank saw her as valuable collateral in his bid to secure a stronghold for British cinema on the postwar world market and was eager to have her on board. The only approval needed was Shaw's. Despite her long run in *The Doctor's Dilemma*, the elderly playwright had never seen Vivien perform and didn't know what she looked like. "It is a curious fact that the ladies who set their eye on that particular role are invariably giantesses of over fifty," he said. His seal of approval was only given when Vivien, thirty years old and standing a petite 5'3", paid a visit to his home in Ayot St. Lawrence, Hertfordshire.

Cameras started rolling at Denham Studios in June 1944. Pascal, who had been successful in adapting Shaw's *Pygmalion* and *Major Barbara* in previous years, was given free reign and an open purse. No expense was spared in the Hungarian director's quest for historical accuracy. Sand was imported from Egypt and a life-size Sphinx created at the studio. Over two thousand extras were employed to fill the replica city of Alexandria, which cost an exorbitant amount of money to build. The sheer extravagance of *Caesar and Cleopatra* was compared to a D. W. Griffith epic and boded well for its perspective competition with Hollywood. However, many in Britain found Pascal's wild expenditure in the midst of wartime austerity tasteless.

Like *Gone With the Wind*, filming *Caesar and Cleopatra* was problematic from the beginning. Air raids and gunfire threatened the months of hard labor that went into building the sets, not to mention the lives of the cast and crew themselves. Script supervisor Marjorie Deans recalled one incident when she and Pascal were nearly blown to pieces by a flying bomb. In his autobiography, costar Stewart Granger wrote of his own near-death experience. While hoisted 150 feet in the air on a crane during the scene where his character Apollodorus presents Caesar with a Persian rug concealing Cleopatra, an unmanned German V1 exploded a mere two hundred yards from the set. "The whole construction started to sway. I yelled out in terror and suddenly some of the men realized what happened. 'Christ, it's old Jim, we've forgotten the poor bugger.'" Dangerous conditions were further impacted by gloomy weather. The use of Technicolor required sunshine for the outdoor scenes and the shooting schedule was constantly delayed by incessant rain.

Vivien was not spared from suffering along with her cast mates. What she had hoped would be a worthy exercise in professional development was hampered by Shaw's lack of understanding of the filmic medium. Pascal had taken liberties with the script of *Pygmalion* in 1938 and thus was denied permission to change or cut any of the original text in subsequent adaptations of the playwright's work. Shaw's insistence that Cleopatra be acted according to his own vision, exactly as written, left Vivien no room for interpretation. Aside from feeling artistically stifled, she was miserable in Oliver Messel's visually stunning costumes. The light-

---

Returning from Africa, Vivien settled with Olivier at Old Prestwick in Gerrards Cross. David Niven and his wife, Primmie, were frequent visitors. Niven took this photo of the Oliviers with their cat, Anna (and kittens).

weight material accurately suggested the heat of the Egyptian desert but did little to ward off the cold that plagued England in the summer and autumn of 1944.

"*What* do you suppose has happened," Vivien wrote to Leigh Holman in August. "I'm to have a baby." She once described the experience of childbirth as "humiliating" and "didn't care for it at all." Nor had she or Olivier assumed active roles as parents to their previous children. But Olivier wanted to be a family man and Vivien was eager to fulfill his aspirations. A mutual child would confirm their love and bind them together for the rest of their lives. The highly emotional passion that had brought them together in the first place made her insecure at the thought that she might lose his affections if she failed to create and sustain an idyllic life for them as a couple. This unwarranted fear made the impending tragedy even harder to bear.

Pascal and the rest of the crew were not as pleased with Vivien's news as she was. "Everyone is very, very cross & keeps asking me how I suppose they are going to make me look like the 16 year Cleopatra & I keep saying I can't help it, that it's an act from God and that they're not to be mean to me in my condition!"

Wanting to "hurry up and finish the film," Vivien went into overdrive. Stewart Granger's wife, Elspeth March, who was expecting a baby of her own at the time, remembered Vivien being hyperactive and unable to get adequate sleep. She also did her own stunts as no body double was employed. While filming the scene where Cleopatra runs through the great hall in the Memphis Palace, leaps over to Caesar who is sitting by her throne and declares herself a real queen, Vivien

lost her footing on the freshly polished studio floor and fell. She miscarried two days later, on August 31—her fourth wedding anniversary.

After a six-week hiatus, Vivien returned to the set and unsuccessfully attempted to have Pascal replaced as director. The remainder of the shoot was an unhappy one and when the film premiered in December 1945 she decided not to attend. It was just as well. *Caesar and Cleopatra* was one of the most successful films of the early postwar period in terms of ticket sales but it failed to make a profit. As soon as the lights came on a feeling of disappointment permeated in the lavishly decorated Odeon Marble Arch. "It is, let's face it, a third-rate, dreary

Vivien and Hungarian director Gabriel Pascal visit playwright George Bernard Shaw at Shaw's Corner in Ayot St. Lawrence. Vivien appeared wearing little makeup and convinced Shaw that she was right for the part of Cleopatra in Pascal's upcoming epic.

play, which yet might have been turned in to a successful movie extravaganza if a completely new script had been written for the screen," wrote Simon Harcourt-Smith in *The Tribune*. C. A. Lejeune found it "a singularly cold triumph." In America, audiences failed to return for repeat viewings. They were promised sex and intrigue but instead paid for two hours of Shavian philosophy and performances that, while deemed "competent and even excellent" by some critics, were easily overshadowed by the spectacle in the background. It was "a Technicolor camel, exotic but not romantic." Seven years would pass before Vivien could bring herself to watch it, and only then because she was acting the part on stage opposite Olivier.

Thornton Wilder's Pulitzer-winning "history of mankind in comic strip" had left American audiences delightfully confused for two years before the script for *The Skin of Our Teeth* fell into Olivier's lap. The absurdist morality play about the fictional Antrobus family of New Jersey had proved successful for Tallulah Bankhead, Miriam Hopkins, Gladys George, and Lizabeth Scott in New York. Vivien fell immediately under the spell of the play's pessimistic but charming heroine. Lily Sabina, the family maid, seductive beauty queen, and narrator, was a complex character and Olivier thought it an ideal showcase for her rarely seen comedic talents. They purchased the British rights in early 1944 and began planning with Binkie Beaumont at H. M. Tennant as soon as Vivien finished work on *Caesar and Cleopatra*. It would be their first director-actress partnership since the disastrous *Romeo and Juliet*.

Soon after rehearsals began, Vivien received a stern letter from Selznick International. She was still under obligation to fulfill her seven-year contract and over the past four years had been politely evading the issue of returning to Hollywood to do more films. Selznick had been temporarily appeased by the large payout he received from the Rank Organization for loaning Vivien out to make *Caesar and Cleopatra*, but he could not allow her to continue appearing in projects that did nothing to benefit his company and financial interests. She was an "exotic plant" that had to be protected from "unwise exposure." When Vivien refused to withdraw from the production, Selznick sought an injunction for breach of contract. Over the next six months, lawyers would battle in the London courts over the future of Vivien's career. It was ruled that her age and marital status subjected her to the possibility of being called up for war service. When it came down to a choice between the play, idleness, or possible work in a factory, Vivien chose to carry on with the play.

The Skin of Our Teeth opened at the Phoenix Theatre shortly after VE Day in May 1945. Audiences were as perplexed in London as they had been in New York. For critics, however, it was an unconventional and eccentric revelation; the best performance Vivien had yet given. James Agate summed up the general critical opinion in his *Sunday Times* review: "Through it all, lovely to look at, flitted and fluttered Miss Leigh's hired girl, Sabina, an enchanting piece of nonsense-cum-allure, half dabchick and half dragonfly. The best performance of its kind since Yvonne Printemps." For the first time in her career, she proved she could carry a complicated play on

Vivien as Shaw's kittenish queen in a publicity photograph for *Caesar and Cleopatra* (1945).

her own. And she had finally managed to free herself from the pervasive notion that she was a beautiful but merely competent stage actress; she was a bona-fide star in her own right.

The play had been running for two months when Vivien's colleagues noticed that she had lost quite a bit of weight and became uncharacteristically tired. Binkie Beaumont took her to see a doctor and she was forced to leave the play when a tubercular patch was discovered on her lung. She had had TB as a child, but she delayed telling Olivier about the diagnosis, for fear she would worry him while he was on an important victory tour in Europe with the Entertainments National Service Association (ENSA). Olivier received confusing secondhand information from Alfred Lunt and Lynn Fontanne in Paris and wrote home imploring for accurate news. "Your sorrow is my worst fear," Olivier told Vivien. "Your life my life."

Vivien required immediate treatment and a long convalescence. Hearing word of her illness in

TOP LEFT: *Caesar and Cleopatra* was not a happy film. Pascal failed to employ a body double for Vivien and she suffered a miscarriage after a fall on the set.

TOP RIGHT: With Claude Rains as Caesar.

RIGHT: Vivien as Lily Sabina, "half dabchick, half dragonfly," in Thornton Wilder's absurd comedy *The Skin of Our Teeth*, 1945.

Hollywood, Selznick put aside their professional differences and with genuine concern offered to pay for her to stay in a sanitarium in Palm Springs or Arizona, where the dry desert air would have her back on her feet in no time. Again she declined his request, preferring to stay in England to be close to Olivier. She checked in to a hospital near Brompton, West London. When her husband returned from the continent, they traveled to the Scottish Highlands for a recuperative holiday before retreating to Notley Abbey, their newly purchased country home in Buckinghamshire.

CHAPTER 4

THEATER ROYALTY

"Her name, combined with that of Sir Laurence Olivier, for twenty years her husband, was the greatest 'draw' of the post-war theater."

—*The Guardian*, July 10, 1967

V ivien had reservations about moving in to Notley Abbey at the war's end. The twelfth-century monastery, built during the reign of Henry II and later endowed by Henry V, was in a state of ruin and in desperate need of repair when the Oliviers came upon it during a house hunt. Vivien thought it depressing at first glance. With inadequate plumbing and drafty rooms, the renovation

would be costly. But Olivier was wholly enchanted by its history. He relished the opportunity to create a private and romantic marital haven away from the hurried demands of London life.

In the late 1950s Vivien would look back on their time at Notley with nostalgic affection, telling her stepson Tarquin that she couldn't "imagine life without such an oasis." During the nine months that she spent in virtual seclusion there, she made it her own and grew to love it as much as her husband did. From her large L-shaped bedroom overlooking the lawn sweeping down to the River

---

The Oliviers stopped by Angus McBean's studio in early 1948 for publicity photos to take to Australia.

The Oliviers occasionally let the press photograph them at home in London, as they did here in 1946.

BOTTOM LEFT: At Durham Cottage in London with Vivien's favorite cat, New Boy.

Thame, she played hostess to her close friends, including David Niven, John and Mary Mills, and Robert Helpmann. When spring arrived and she was allowed out of bed, she often busied herself in the rose garden, taking pleasure in giving new life to the overgrown landscape. Renée Asherson, who acted with Olivier in *Henry V* and who would later play Stella to Vivien's Blanche in the London production of *A Streetcar Named Desire*, recalls to this day the pleasure of being invited to Notley on occasion. She and Vivien would do the shopping together in the nearby village of Long Crendon, where Vivien would shed her celebrity image and make small talk with the locals.

What Vivien wanted most, however, was prevented by her ill health. When her doctors forbade her to try for another baby, she focused her maternal attention on Olivier's son. Tarquin was ten in the summer of 1946 and barely knew his father, having only just returned from California the year before. He treasured weekends at Notley. Vivien encouraged him to play the piano and made him feel that his adolescent interests "were precisely the things which interested her too." Most significantly, she helped to forge something of a connection between father and son. "She, whose passion had deprived me of my father, did all she could to bring us together."

In a gesture reminiscent to that of the nuns at the Convent of the Sacred Heart, Olivier presented her with a cat called New Boy to bring comfort to Vivien during periods of loneliness. The seal point Siamese, named after the London theater where Olivier had risen to great success, quickly became one of Vivien's most beloved companions. He wore a belled collar from Paris, later accompanied her to

Vivien Leigh with her friend Robert Helpmann at Notley Abbey, circa 1951. Although she had reservations about moving in to the fifteenth-century house at the end of the war, Vivien soon grew to love it as much as Olivier did.

the theater for good luck, and was even photographed for a feature in the *Illustrated London News* showcasing famous cats and their famous owners. With New Boy by her side, Vivien spent much of her free time immersed in the printed word. One of the many books she consumed in her solitude was William Winwood Reade's *The Martyrdom of Man*. It contained a passage that she held close for the rest of her life: "And the artists shall inherit the earth and the world will be as a garden."

The slow nature of Vivien's recovery was a source of concern for Olivier, who worried that she

TOP RIGHT: The Oliviers check in at the airport in London en route to New York with the Old Vic, May 1946.

TOP LEFT: Sleeping on the flight to New York, May 1946.

ABOVE: The Oliviers with Gertrude Lawrence and Alexander Cadogan, British delegate to the U.N., at the Coffee House Club in New York City, May 7, 1946.

RIGHT: Vivien waves to fans from the back seat of a car in New York, May 1946.

might be suffering from something other than a clear-cut case of tuberculosis. Members of the press were also inquisitive about the state of her health. In February 1946, Olivier responded with a private letter to Stephen Watts of the *Sunday Express*, thanking him for his heartfelt concern. Vivien's trouble, he revealed, was more of a mystery than they originally thought and getting conclusive answers from doctors was frustratingly difficult. Vivien had hoped to return to work in May, but Olivier wasn't sure she would be well enough. Her miscarriage the year before sent her into a state of depression, and the uncanny mood swings she had been experiencing sporadically for some time now seemed to occur with more frequency. Unbeknownst to anyone at the time, these were manifestations of the manic depression that would wreak havoc on her life in later years. Alec Guinness, if never an intimate friend, was certainly an astute observer. He remembered hearing whispers of concern about Vivien's mental wellbeing as far back as 1937, when he understudied Olivier in *Hamlet*:

"I never saw cruelty or coldness in Vivien—even her ambitions and her needs were dealt with charmingly and sweetly, insofar as my witness can bear. It was very sad. She appeared, at a very young age, to turn into a lovely stalk of chalk, and the chipping away had begun, and you were there to see the flaking off.

"So many of us, I can attest, tried to do what we could, but there was—and is—nothing really to do. The destiny that gave her that extraordinary beauty and that talent and that magic that surrounded her came, I hate to think, with some exorbitant debts, and those debts were collected early and bluntly and swiftly."

The Oliviers stand in line to greet the Queen at the first Royal Command film performance at the Empire Leicester Square, 1946. The film being shown was Powell and Pressburger's *A Matter of Life and Death*.

Vivien studies her script for *Anna Karenina*, 1947.

As Tolstoy's doomed heroine in *Anna Karenina*. Costumes by Cecil Beaton.

Vivien's long absence from the spotlight corresponded with the meteoric rise of Olivier's stage career. Along with Ralph Richardson, Tyrone Guthrie, and John Burrell, he had been responsible for the revival of the Old Vic Company in 1944. His performance as Richard III in the 1944-45 season helped establish him as the most popular and respected dramatic actor of his generation. Olivier cited the financial burdens of refurbishing Notley and Vivien's medical expenses as the reasons why he felt compelled to take on so much work during this period. Vivien was proud of Olivier's achievements and always spoke of him as the greatest actor in the world. "There's nothing my husband can't do," she would say. Up to this point they had been more or less on equal footing, both striving for excellence on stage. Now, Vivien worried that as Olivier ascended to the heights while she remained idle, his love for his characters and the personal rewards of success had begun to eclipse his love for her.

In May 1946 her doctors gave Vivien permission to travel with Olivier to New York, where the Old Vic Company performed a short season of repertory. Their arrival was covered by Radie Harris

LEFT: Philippe Halsman photographed Vivien for the cover of *LIFE* magazine in New York in the spring of 1946. She disliked his photographs and tore up his prints, including this one, which was never published. But Olivier loved what he saw of the contacts and urged Halsman to submit his work for publication.

TOP RIGHT: The final scene of *Anna Karenina* was enhanced by Henri Alekan's stunning black-and-white cinematography.

RIGHT: Waiting to shoot the scene where Anna watches Vronsky at the races.

in *Photoplay*. According to the journalist, Vivien looked beautiful and well, and was in high demand from her friends and film studios. *Saratoga Trunk*, *A Portrait of Jennie*, and *Forever Amber* were but three of the high-profile titles on offer. Of *Forever Amber* Vivien was reported to have said, "I'm told that Darryl Zanuck offered me a million dollars to take over the role. If he has, it's all news to me. I wish he had. I'd feel so elegant turning down a million dollars!"

While her fans were reassured that she was completely well again, others who came into contact with Vivien in New York told a different story. Philippe Halsman was one of several people who experienced the duality of Vivien's personality dur-

ing this time. The photographer, best known for his portraits of celebrities jumping in mid-air, was commissioned by *LIFE* magazine to photograph Vivien as promotion for the U.S. release of *Caesar and Cleopatra*. He had admired her since *Gone With the Wind* and upon first meeting thought her "exquisite, she was full of gentile charm and friendliness and at the end of the sitting I had the feeling that I was photographing something very unusual: an angel-like star." The developed prints did not reveal the same beauty he had seen

---

Vivien and Alexander Korda are visited by Cary Grant on the set of *Anna Karenina*.

through the lens. Instead, they showed a tired and sick woman. She agreed to leave her sickbed for another sitting and Halsman was so impressed by her professionalism that he broke his own rule of not showing photos to his sitters before publication. Happy with the results of the second session, he brought his new prints around to the St. Regis Hotel at Vivien's request.

As Halsman showed Vivien the skillfully developed photographs, her expression changed from happiness to one of anger. The photographs were terrible, she said, threatening to ruin his career if he published them against her wishes. He described his disappointment when Vivien proceeded to destroy hours of hard work in front of his eyes. Later that evening, the Oliviers's mutual agent, Cecil Tennant phoned Halsman to say that although she had torn up the prints, Vivien had left the contact sheets in the envelope. Olivier saw the delicate beauty captured by Halsman's expert eye and urged him to submit them for publication. One photo, showing Vivien in three-quarter profile and looking directly at the camera, made a successful cover.

After *Gone With the Wind*, prestigious costume dramas emerged as Vivien's forte. In early 1947, she signed on to star in Korda's highly anticipated remake of Tolstoy's *Anna Karenina*. Like J. Arthur Rank, Korda was eager to reestablish his films overseas once the war ended. *Anna Karenina* was his most ambitious and costly film on offer for 1948. As part of his plan for international appeal, Korda assembled an acclaimed European crew that included French director Julien Duvivier, cinematographer Henri Alekan, and Russian art director André Andrejew to make the sets. Duvivier and playwright Jean Anouilh were assigned to bring

new life to Tolstoy's revered classic, but their idea of staging the story in contemporary France met with such disapproval that Korda brought in British journalist Guy Morgan to help transport the plot back to its original setting in nineteenth-century Russia.

Vivien traveled to Paris with designer Cecil Beaton in May. While being fitted for costumes for the film, she received a call from Olivier in London. He had been named in the King's birthday honors list to receive a knighthood for his services to the British theater. Vivien would cling to her title as Lady Olivier until her dying day, but at present the news brought out mixed emotions. Pride for his stature mingled with lingering indignation at having not been cast in her husband's art house film version of *Hamlet*. In the past, she and Olivier had both publicly disapproved of filming Shakespeare, but *Henry V* helped Olivier realize his own artistic potential as an actor-director. His change of attitude influenced Vivien's own. Olivier had been full of admiration for her Ophelia at Elsinore ten years earlier. Although she was no longer a supporting actress and Ophelia would not have done much for her career, she still wanted to work alongside her husband. To be denied the role now because either he or Rank's financial backers thought her too old cut Vivien deeply. Her disappointment worsened when Olivier chose to cast seventeen-year-old Jean Simmons, who bore an uncanny resemblance to Vivien in her younger years. Simmons had never attempted Shakespeare before, and her only notable film performance to that date was as young Estella in David Lean's *Great Expectations*.

"You won't take it, of course?" Vivien said over the phone. Whether she was joking or not is unclear. Olivier seemed to assume she was and

immediately wrote to accept the honor, but Beaton noted Vivien's displeased mood when he came into her dressing room to offer his congratulations. She was disdainful, saying she thought the honor ridiculous. "The leading lady, so carefree and intelligent in her private life, becomes entirely different when the strain of picture making begins to tell," Beaton observed.

Trouble on the set of *Anna Karenina* contributed to Vivien's unhappiness. Korda originally wanted Olivier to play Anna's dashing lover Count Vronsky. Due to his unavailability the producer played a wildcard and cast relatively unknown Irish actor Kieron Moore. Alexander Walker described Moore as one of the most promising young actors in British cinema at the time, but he was no match for his leading lady in either talent or temperament

and their lack of chemistry is palpable on screen. So poorly miscast was Moore that some critics at the film's London premiere were overheard referring to him as "Moron Kier." Vivien also disagreed with Ralph Richardson's portrayal of Anna's cold, aristocratic husband. Richardson was a close friend of Olivier's and Vivien knew him well outside of work. However, she felt he played Karenin too sympathetically, thereby lessening the credibility of Anna's affair with Vronsky and her eventual suicide. Tarquin Olivier recalled visiting Vivien at Shepper-

In October 1947, Olivier, aged forty, became Britain's youngest actor-knight. He and Vivien were photographed arriving at Buckingham Palace for the ceremony.

The Oliviers attend the royal premiere of *The Bishop's Wife* at the Empire Leicester Square, 1947.

ton Studios and being allowed to watch the daily rushes. "What do you think of him?" Vivien asked, referring to Richardson. Tarquin thought him nice. "Exactly, and that's quite wrong," said Vivien. "He should be a brute."

"I know about Anna," Vivien told Richardson's wife, Muriel Forbes. "I was inside her. I know everything about her, and yet they say I can't do it." In constructing her own portrayal, Vivien wanted to convey Anna's driving obsession and the nature of her love for Vronsky, rather than glorifying her tragic ending. She knew she could bring some-

thing raw to the story of an aristocratic woman trapped in a loveless marriage and forced to choose between her passion for another man and her love for her son. She understood the emotions that motivated Tolstoy's greatest heroine—the visceral passion, the feeling of guilt at having left her child—because she was living it with Olivier. On this point she clashed heavily with Duvivier. She was used to getting her own way, but with Korda in America for most of the shoot, there was no one on hand to support her argument. Duvivier held little regard for Anna as a character and was mainly

interested in creating a somber mood in the film. His obstinacy played a large role in influencing the tepid reception of both Vivien's performance and the film in general.

In keeping with the trend of praising austere theatricality, Ralph Richardson received the most laurels. On both sides of the Atlantic, many critics seemed unable to assess Vivien without thinking of Greta Garbo, who had played Anna twice on screen before. She was beautiful and magnetic, they said, but too removed, lacking the depth and warmth displayed in Clarence Brown's 1935 film. Although Vivien admired Garbo as an actress, she wasn't amused by the constant comparisons between Garbo's performances and her own. "No one can top Garbo," she tersely replied when the *Los Angeles Times* mentioned the difficulty of filling the reclusive Swedish star's shoes. When asked whether she had seen either the 1927 or the 1935 versions, Vivien admitted that she hadn't. It was dangerous to get too familiar with another actor's characterization when attempting the same role. Terence Rattigan felt that Vivien "could act love and acted, as she acted all things, with brilliance, dedication, and artistry, but somehow her Anna Karenina didn't quite show the quality that it should have."

Vivien's name alone was enough to sell tickets

TOP: The Old Vic company arrives in Freemantle for the start of their Australian tour, March 1948.

MIDDLE: At one of many official functions in Australia, 1948.

BOTTOM: The Oliviers were photographed everywhere in Australia. A glimpse of them walking down the street was enough to cause a stir with eager fans.

overseas and *Anna Karenina* probably would have been more commercially successful had its release not coincided with the Anglo-American film war. In August 1947, Sir Stafford Cripps, president of the British Board of Trade, placed a heavy import duty on American films. It was hoped that the tariff would inspire more impressive homegrown products and prevent the Hollywood industry from gaining complete control of their domestic market as the postwar economy went into a tailspin. Hollywood boycotted, making it difficult for British producers to exhibit their films in American cinemas well into 1948. According to Martin Stockham, when Korda was asked what percentage of the overseas profits was lost because of the embargo, he replied, "One hundred percent."

While engaged in their respective film projects in 1947, the Oliviers accepted an invitation from the British Council to act as actor-ambassadors and lead the Old Vic Company on a nine-month tour of Australia and New Zealand. The aim was to spread goodwill and introduce the Antipodes to the best of British theater. Olivier handpicked the cast members, planning to use the tour as tryouts for a prospective National Theatre Company. Many, including Terence Morgan and Peter Cushing, had previously appeared in his films and plays. Vivien was glad to finally reassume an equal position as the star alongside her husband. The program consisted of *Richard III*, *The Skin of Our Teeth*, and Richard Brinsley Sheridan's *The School for Scandal*; two plays to showcase their individual strengths

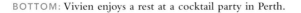

TOP: Taking a much-needed break at Scarborough Beach in Perth.

BOTTOM: Vivien enjoys a rest at a cocktail party in Perth.

The Oliviers visit with the University of Western Australia Dramatic Society after a performance of *Oedipus the King*.

Congratulating the players of *Oedipus the King* on a job well done.

and one to highlight their combined talents.

The night before their departure, Vivien and Olivier threw a glittering party at Durham Cottage for seventy of their friends. Vivien had a reputation for being a great hostess and took pride in creating an atmosphere of meticulous perfection, a trait learned from her mother. "When I was a little girl and I was going to a party," she told David Lewin, "my mother always said, 'Now do what the host wants, to please him,' and when I was the hostess my mother used to say, 'Now do what the guests want, to please them.' And I asked, 'When can I do what I want?' Not doing what you want is good manners."

In the years to come, Vivien's parties would take on a legendary aura. Olivier's date book from 1950

gives a good indication of the illustrious figures of stage and screen that regularly visited Notley: husky-voiced character actor Roger Livesey, his wife Ursula Jeans, and her sister Isabel, who had starred with Vivien in *The Happy Hypocrite*. There was Alexander Korda, Michael Redgrave and Rachel Kempson, Robert Helpmann, and the journalist Alan Dent. Hollywood stars like Olivia de Havilland, Marlene Dietrich, Katharine Hepburn, Danny Kaye, Orson Welles, and Judy Garland found themselves at Notley whenever they visited England. Vivien's family also came on occasion, as did Jill Esmond and Tarquin. Peter Finch sensed an atmosphere of bitterness among people who weren't lucky enough to be invited: "An attitude circulated that these weekend parties were in some way exclusive gatherings of a small and somewhat superior theatrical clique. It was never like that. Vivien adored her home and she was never happier than when she could share the peace and beauty of Notley."

After an evening's performance in London, guests would climb into their cars for the fifty-mile journey to Notley Abbey. The blazing lights emanating from the stone mansion penetrated the dark countryside as they made their way down the long drive lined with walnut and lime trees, one of Olivier's personal touches. No matter how late people arrived, there would always be an elaborate meal served to Vivien's high standards. English food was too heavy for her tastes. She preferred her cuisine to be cooked in the French style. Although her drink of choice was a gin and tonic, she and Olivier were both connoisseurs of vintage wines and kept the cellar well stocked. Dinner would be followed by dessert, coffee, and port before everyone retired to the drawing room for ribald conversation and light entertainment—Chinese checkers, quiz games, dancing around the gramophone—that lasted into the early hours of the morning. On nearly every occasion, Vivien remained awake and full of energy long after even the heartiest partygoer had gone to bed.

The Oliviers's 1948 Australian tour was a major cultural event that lived on in the minds of both

TOP: With the Vice Chancellor of the University of Western Australia.

RIGHT: "Two walking corpses" greet the press upon their arrival back in England after a successful but thoroughly exhausting tour, November 1948.

actors and audience members long after the final curtain fell. Their reputation preceded them. Actor Michael Blakemore was a medical student in Sydney at the time and remembers the air of excitement when two of the world's most distinguished stars announced an extended visit to the island nation: "We all thought it was like a present for helping win the war. They had this world celebrity because before television, the movies sort of swept round the globe like an epidemic, like a virus. And these initial stars—the Clark Gables, the Gary Coopers, the Laurence Oliviers, the Vivien Leighs—they occupied enormous space in the collective minds of the population."

For many, seeing the Oliviers in person was the event of a lifetime and not an opportunity to be missed. After a month-long voyage that took them first to Cape Town for two days of sightseeing, the company opened in Perth on March 20, 1948. Those lucky enough to attend the opening night performance of *The School for Scandal* at the Capitol Theatre treated it as a grand occasion, turning out in evening gowns, white tie, and tails. In Sydney, one couple were married at 6:00 and cut their wedding reception short to make it to the Tivoli Theatre in time for an 8 p.m. performance of *Richard III*. Another fan, Darwin Health Department employee Eileen Joseph, was so desperate to see the company perform that she took leave from her job and traveled two thousand miles to Adelaide. Her dedication was rewarded with a complimentary ticket and a personal meeting with Vivien and Olivier in their dressing room. Many eager fans queued overnight for tickets. In Melbourne, a seventy-five-year-old woman slept outside in the rain to get a seat in the upper circle for *Scandal*. "I

would gladly do it again," *The Age* reported her as saying. "It was worth every penny." The show attracted an audience of 1,600, drawing comparisons to a League final match at the Melbourne Cricket Ground.

King George VI and Queen Elizabeth were scheduled to make an appearance in Australia the following year and it was thought that some Aussies treated the Old Vic visit as a dress rehearsal for the real thing. The Oliviers anticipated fanfare, but nothing had prepared them for the intrusive level of adulation that awaited them. Australia and New Zealand proved to be a combined microcosm of celebrity culture that played a large role in transforming them into living legends. In the Antipodes they weren't thought of as mere film stars, they were "a first gentleman and lady of the British stage and screen . . . the Prince Charming and lovely princess of every fairytale." Vivien was of particular interest to Australian women, and was thought of as a paragon of beauty, glamour, taste, and decorum. During her many public appearances, she was asked by women's magazines to give her opinion on everything from Christian Dior's "New Look," to Australian wine, and the state of rationing in England. In answer to a question about her favorite film star, she chose Garbo, but only after she was forced to discount Olivier.

From the moment the H. M. S. *Corinthic* docked in the harbor at Freemantle, fans and photographers besieged the Oliviers, determined to follow and document their every move. Michael Redington was one of the youngest members of the company.

Theatre Royalty, 1948.

At the premiere of the John Mills film *Scott of the Antarctic*, London, 1948.

"There's never been anything like it," he said. "The crowds at the stage door . . . When we left each town, there were always busses to take us from the theater to the station or the theater to the airport. You couldn't move. I remember those busses took *hours* to get away." Vivien and Olivier were "absolutely at their height. These two great stars and then all of us around them. . . . He went everywhere and he was marvelous, and he spoke beautifully. And there beside him, looking up at him, was this most beautiful woman, dressed exquisitely and always giving to him." So respected were the Oliviers by the rest of the company that they acquired the nickname "God and the Angel."

In nearly every city from Perth to Hobart, the company performed to standard, with Vivien receiving resounding praise for her deft artistry and command of both Sabina in *The Skin of Our Teeth* and Lady Teazle in *The School for Scandal*. But by June, the Oliviers had begun to buckle under the strain of their grueling schedule and the relentless pursuit by the press. In Melbourne, both actors were forced to let their understudies take over for several days due to illness. Vivien publicly admitted her exhaustion and her doctors ordered her to cut back on social appearances. Olivier condemned the "shocking state of affairs," saying, "it must never happen again." But however much they pleaded for rest and relaxation, privacy was nowhere to be found. Newspapers took pleasure in reporting the couple's whereabouts ahead of their arrival, often forcing them to hastily change plans and travel incognito. When the company reached Sydney, Vivien desperately told the *Morning Herald*, "If we don't have peace and quiet here we will have to return to Tasmania or even Darwin." What

was supposed to have been a secret hotel stay in Surfer's Paradise was cut short by lingering, voyeuristic fans hoping for a celebrity sighting.

"You may not know it, but you're talking to two walking corpses," Olivier told reporters when the *Corinthic* pulled in to Tilbury. The company returned to England in mid-November, triumphant but thoroughly exhausted. When asked if there was any chance of a repeat visit down under in the foreseeable future, Vivien quickly dismissed the idea, saying the social schedule had been too heavy even for her tastes. "Why, we saw practically nothing of the country except its theaters. . . . It was anything but a rest cure."

On a personal level, the Australian tour marked a crucial turning point in the Oliviers's relationship. As their legendary reputation firmly took hold of the public imagination, cracks began to appear beneath the surface. Terence Morgan's wife, Georgina Jumel, was Vivien's understudy and recalled that although the couple never showed anything but happiness and positivity in front of the rest of the cast, by the end of the tour "something had cooled between them." Indeed, Olivier later wrote that he felt he had lost Vivien in Australia. Shortly after their return, she told him she was no longer in love with him; that she saw him now as more of a brother than a lover. There was no one else, she explained, and a divorce would not be necessary.

It was difficult for Olivier to comprehend or fully believe that he and Vivien were no longer on the same page when it came to their feelings for one another. "It had always been inconceivable that this great, this glorious passion could ever not exist," he later wrote. Vivien's lifelong reverence for

Olivier (her doctors were more blunt, referring to it as a "pathological obsession") has made her confession somewhat difficult to analyze. From the beginning, passionate lust had been a mainstay of their relationship. Now that the sexual compatibility had cooled, Olivier still seemed content but Vivien found herself at a loss. If her husband could no longer satisfy her needs, she wanted to, and eventually did, look elsewhere for fulfillment. Yet, at the same time, their marriage was precious to her. Whatever else may happen, she believed that their bond was indestructible. Ultimately, neither was willing to disillusion the public by shattering their image as an iconic romantic couple.

While in Australia, Olivier received word that he had been dismissed from his post as actor-manager at the Old Vic. Despite two successful seasons and undeniable prestige, the Board of Directors decided that Olivier and Ralph Richardson could either be actors, splitting their time between stage and screen, or they could be full-time theater directors. Not both. Olivier was outraged, but took the opportunity to strike out on his own as an independent actor-director, focusing on expanding Vivien's stage career.

Olivier's contract with the Old Vic finished in January 1949 with a short season at the New Theatre. The program of *Richard III*, *The School for Scandal*, and a modern dress version of *Antigone* adapted by Jean Anouilh marked the first time he and Vivien had acted together on the British stage. *Antigone* was Vivien's idea. She didn't care much for either of the other characters she was playing. Lady Anne in *Richard III* was a small and rather thankless part. She considered Lady Teazle too superficial, despite Olivier and many critics thinking her perfectly suited for it. Having proved herself a skillful light comedienne, she was now eager to conquer tragedy. *Antigone* also served as an unofficial audition. Sitting in the audience was American playwright Tennessee Williams, in town searching for an actress to play Blanche DuBois in the London production of his controversial play *A Streetcar Named Desire*.

Vivien with Dan Cunningham in Jean Anouilh's adaptation of Sophocles' *Antigone*, 1949.

CHAPTER 5

STREETCAR

"Vivien's Blanche . . . was certainly one of the most harrowing things I have ever seen in any theatre anywhere. In trying to tear at my heartstrings, she certainly tore at her own."

—Tennessee Williams

A *Streetcar Named Desire* crashed onto Broadway in 1947, earning Tennessee Williams a Pulitzer Prize for fiction and making an instant star of Marlon Brando. Set in the sweltering atmosphere of postwar New Orleans, it is the story of Blanche DuBois, a fading Southern belle who goes to live with her sister Stella after their family estate, Belle Reve, is buried under a mountain of debt. Plagued by alcoholism, frayed nerves, and a sexual past she desperately but unsuccessfully tries to outrun, Blanche's fragile grip on her own sanity crumbles when she comes up against the primitive brutality of Stella's husband, Stanley Kowalski. Cecil Beaton saw the play in New York and alerted Vivien to its genius. She took the script with her to Australia in 1948 and it didn't take long for her to become convinced that Williams's delicate and wounded heroine was exceptional.

It was Vivien's personality, rather than her acting, that intrigued Tennessee Williams. He came to London with Irene Mayer Selznick, who was coproducing the London production with Binkie Beaumont. They went to the theater daily. "Vivien Leigh is not really good in *Antigone*," he wrote to his friend Donald Windham on May 8, 1949, "but I have a feeling, now, that she might make a good Blanche, more from her offstage personality than what she does in repertory, though she is quite good in

---

Angus McBean captured Vivien with his camera in 1949. Vivien bleached her hair blonde for the play.

School for Scandal. She has great charm." After viewing three performances at the New Theatre the deal was set in stone and the contracts signed over dinner at Beaumont's house. Shortly afterward, the Oliviers honored Williams with a weekend party at Notley Abbey. Selznick and Williams's partner, Frank Merlo, were also invited. Vivien's kindness toward Merlo was most appreciated. Later, in 1963, when Merlo was dying of lung cancer, Vivien threw a party and made Merlo the guest of honor. "Vivien centered the whole dinner party around him with an intuitive sympathy that will always endear her memory to me," Williams recorded in his memoirs. "She did it without seeming to do it. . . . Having known madness, she knew how it was to be draw-

ing close to death." Williams would come to admire her talents as an actress over time, but her friendship was immediate and cherished.

Rehearsals for *Streetcar* began on August 29, 1949. From the beginning, Vivien found herself in the middle of a clash of wills. Elia Kazan had directed the Broadway version and worked closely with Irene Selznick and Williams in terms of staging and honoring the playwright's integrity. Selznick hoped she would have the same luck with Olivier as director; that Vivien and the rest of the cast would benefit immensely from collaborating with Williams. This was not to be the case. In her memoirs, Selznick recounted her frustration in working with Olivier. She was put off by what she saw as his egotism and need for total control—something she, being the daughter of movie mogul Louis B. Mayer and former wife of producer David O. Selznick, liked to exert herself. What irritated Selznick most was Olivier's nonchalance about defying Williams's wish that no cuts be made to the text without his explicit permission. "He said, 'Oh, the old boy won't mind. Why should he? Surely it is a director's prerogative to take out anything he wants to and rearrange as he sees fit."

Selznick believed Olivier was letting his elevated position in the London theater get to his head, and chalked his attitude up to a dislike and misunderstanding of the play. However, a lengthy letter written by Olivier to Tennessee Williams from the Midland Hotel during the trial run in Manchester reveals that his principal reason for manipulat-

---

Antigone acted as an unofficial audition for Vivien. Sitting in on several performances was playwright Tennessee Williams, who was looking for an actress to star in the London production of *A Streetcar Named Desire.*

ing the text was Vivien. Olivier thought *Streetcar* "really great" but never would have chosen to direct it had Vivien not been so determined to act in it. Some of their friends believed it a mistake to play a character that hit so close to home, and for Olivier to encourage it given his long-standing knowledge of her mental fragility. But history had proven that once Vivien set her heart on something, there was no turning back, and Olivier stood behind her. "Everyone said I was mad to try it. They are often saying I am mad to try things," Vivien confessed. "But Blanche is such a real part, the truth about a woman with everything stripped away. She is a tragic figure and I understand her." It was also a psychologically dangerous part, but one that had the potential to distinguish Vivien as

a respected dramatic actress once and for all. She needed the support of a director whom she trusted, and there was no one she trusted more than Olivier.

Streetcar had been well received in New York, but Olivier worried that London would see it as not just an American play, but a foreign one. Even with mandatory censorship by the Lord Chamberlain, the West End would be unprepared for a play that

dealt unambiguously with sexuality. Olivier had enough experience in front of and behind the curtain to know what power critics held over audiences. Bernard Braden played Mitch and remembered Olivier saying, "If the critics lead the audience in the wrong direction, the wrong people will come to see it, for the wrong reasons." Olivier bluntly told Williams that certain scenes in the play

were too long, "repetitious," and "overwritten." Sympathy needed to remain with Vivien/Blanche throughout, and the audience had to be manipulated so they wouldn't lose focus or interest. Vivien shared her husband's feelings in this respect, but she felt that unnecessary cutting of essential lines would destroy the true meaning of the play.

To Vivien, *Streetcar* was a Greek tragedy in modern form, and this could not be properly conveyed without keeping the intricate layers of Williams's text in tact. She was the only cast member who occasionally argued with Olivier if she felt the situation warranted it. Bernard Braden suspected that Vivien usually gave in to her husband's obstinacy because she was aware of her own limitations and depended on Olivier's expertise to shape her performance. "When he gave her a direction that she knew was wrong for the play, she couldn't be certain if he was giving that direction simply because he didn't understand, or to find a

LEFT: Olivier congratulates Vivien on her successful performance in *A Streetcar Named Desire* at the Aldwych Theatre, London, 1949. Although the play caused much controversy, Vivien received a standing ovation on the opening night.

BOTTOM LEFT: 1950 publicity shot for *A Streetcar Named Desire*.

BOTTOM RIGHT: Director William Wyler greets Vivien, Olivier, and Vivien's daughter, Suzanne, on their arrival at the airport in Los Angeles, 1950. Wyler was to direct Olivier in *Carrie*.

ABOVE: At a tailgate picnic in Los Angeles, 1950.

BELOW: Giving a radio broadcast with Hollywood gossip columnist Louella Parsons, 1950. Vivien seemed to prefer Louella to her rival Hedda Hopper.

way around her inadequacies."

Shortly before the trial run, Irene Selznick called a mandatory meeting with Olivier and Beaumont. Vivien came along uninvited and listened to Selznick talk about correcting the damage Olivier was inflicting on the play and, subsequently, her performance. It was a "bruising experience" for all involved.

Some of the cuts were restored by the time the play opened in Manchester at the beginning of October, but it became apparent early on that the coming months would be considerably challenging for Vivien. The Manchester Opera House was a cavernous theater and actors required great vocal power to reach the entire audience. Although she took regular lessons, Vivien's voice had always been one of her weaknesses. Olivier called a full dress rehearsal on the afternoon before the first performance and by the beginning of the third act, Vivien was "showing such signs of exhaustion" that it became cause for concern. The smaller Aldwych Theatre in London provided some relief, but after six months Vivien was so emotionally and physically depleted that her doctors ordered her to reduce the amount of performances to four per week. Her contract was consequently extended to make up for any lost revenue.

In London, performances sold out immediately, as was now the standard for Leigh-Olivier collaborations. Vivien received a standing ovation on the first night. However, the public reaction toward the play itself was exactly as the Oliviers had feared. Many were unable to accept *Streetcar* as anything other than salacious sensationalism. "Every night when I played it in London the reaction from the audience was awful because they saw it just as something unpleasant about sex," Vivien said, disappointedly. "English people perhaps are so sexually repressed that the play may have brought out the worst in them." Noël Coward went to see it with Joyce Carey and thought Vivien "magnificent," but the audience was "sordid and the theater beastly." John Gielgud agreed, reporting to Alfred Lunt and Lynn Fontanne in America that "the audiences who come and pack in are rather like expectant apes. A pity, but I think it's something to do with the misunderstanding of the Old South, which is Tennessee's strongest poetical postcard . . ."

Vivien found one incident particularly offensive. Bernard Braden was scheduled to do a guest spot on Gracie Fields's radio program, *Our Gracie's Working Party,* and, at Vivien's insistence, invited the comedienne to attend a performance of *Streetcar.* She had never forgotten Fields's encouragement when they worked together for Basil Dean on *Look Up and Laugh* back in 1935. Vivien looked forward to repaying the favor and impressing her former costar. She would "arrange it to suit Gracie. Any night . . . any night at all."

Fields didn't think *Streetcar* would be her sort of play, but Braden managed to persuade her to come to a Saturday showing with a friend. Afterward, Braden found Fields in his dressing room writing a note to Vivien. "I was right, love," she told him. "It wasn't my cup of tea. I thought you were all lovely, and that's what I'm saying in this note. Would you be kind enough to deliver it for me?" Fields left without stopping by to visit Vivien. Braden, too frightened to tell Vivien what had transpired, slipped the note under her door. "What I didn't know was that Vivien had laid on lobster and champagne for Gracie Fields." The slight was not taken lightly. When they met before the performance the following Tuesday, Vivien quietly informed Braden, "I don't think much of your friend's manners."

The unseemly reaction of West End audiences didn't diminish Vivien's admiration for *Streetcar.* When she was offered the chance to reprise Blanche in the Hollywood film version, she accepted without hesitation. Having embodied Blanche for 326 grueling performances, Vivien left for America at the beginning of August 1950. From New York, she traveled cross-country on the *Super Chief,* the pride of the Atchison, Topeka, and Santa Fe Railway. Olivier followed a week later, signing

One of art director Richard Day's set design sketches featuring Blanche DuBois in the opening scene of Elia Kazan's film version of *Streetcar.*

on to star in William Wyler's film adaptation of Theodore Dreiser's novel *Sister Carrie* at Paramount.

It was the Oliviers's first visit to California since taking Hollywood by storm ten years earlier. Rather than fading into obscurity, their activities overseas had created around them an esteemed aura that impressed journalists and fellow actors alike. Vivien was still beautiful, the press were happy to report, and her relationship with Olivier was "one of the most romantic in the theater . . . they did such wonderful work during the war and have worked out their lives so sensibly that now there is nothing but love, affection and feeling of admiration for them." To herald their return, Danny Kaye and his wife, Sylvia Fine, threw a $400 a plate dinner party at the Beverly Hills Hotel. According to Lucinda Ballard, who designed Vivien's costumes for *Streetcar*, the small but exclusive affair was the hottest ticket in town and "people were almost threatening to commit suicide at Vivien's feet if they were not invited." Vivien's daughter, Suzanne, then sixteen and enjoying her first-ever trip to Hollywood stayed home. So did *Los Angeles Times* gossip maven Hedda Hopper, whose negative presumptions about an English girl playing Scarlett O'Hara back in 1939 apparently never sat well with Vivien.

Invitations to parties, dinners, and dances

flooded the mailbox at producer Charles K. Feldman's house in Coldwater Canyon, where the Oliviers stayed for the duration of their trip. Their working schedules were so busy that they preferred quiet get-togethers on weekends. Sundays usually found them at Clifton Webb's place on Rexford Drive in Beverly Hills, enjoying the actor's famous luncheons in the company of Reginald Gardiner, Joan Bennett, Feldman, and two long-time admirers but recently acquired friends, Lauren Bacall and Humphrey Bogart. Feldman's ex-wife, actress-turned-photographer Jean Howard, was often on hand to capture the stars at play. In a photographic retrospective she had published in 1989,

LEFT: Publicity portrait of Vivien for *Streetcar*, taken by stills photographer Bert Six, 1950.

TOP RIGHT: Vivien and director Elia Kazan initially found working with one another difficult, but their collaboration resulted in one of Vivien's best screen performances.

RIGHT: A party on the set of *Streetcar* with director Elia Kazan, Vivien, and actor Nick Dennis. Karl Malden can be seen smiling in the background.

Howard explained the impact the Oliviers had on the Hollywood community: "There was never a more romantic and professional acting team than Vivien Leigh and Laurence Olivier. They epitomized ideal love to many of us. . . . It's sad that they could not have had a happier, healthier life together; Vivien's depressions brought great suffering to both of them."

Vivien had started work on *Streetcar* before reaching Los Angeles. Elia "Gadge" Kazan traveled with her on the train from New York. They spent the entire journey going over the script and discussing Production Code regulations. Unlike Olivier's experience in London, Kazan had been free to stage the play as written in New York. Changes would now have to be considered in

ABOVE: Vivien, in costume as Blanche DuBois, watches the action from behind the camera.

RIGHT: Vivien and Marlon Brando enact the suggested but still controversial rape scene between Stanley Kowalski and Blanche DuBois.

order to get the go-ahead from Hollywood's master censor, Joseph Breen. Thus, Blanche's rape by Stanley is merely hinted at. Any mention of the crux of Blanche's frazzled mental state—her young, dead husband's homosexuality—was eliminated altogether. And Stanley gets his comeuppance at the end of the film.

The changes didn't seem to bother Vivien as

Two rare shots of Vivien fixing her hair on set.

much as they had during the London stage production. By now she was used to working around censorship, saying, "some things have to be conveyed
implicitly rather than explicitly, but I think without
any invidious compromise either way." Kazan was
more outspoken, taking out a page in *The New York
Times* to lambast the Legion of Decency, the organization aimed at making "dirty pictures" suitable for
audiences, and one that held considerable power
over Hollywood. It didn't help Kazan's cause, but it
no doubt generated ticket sales. After the film's
release, Warner Bros. deleted a further five minutes
of footage that dealt with Blanche's promiscuity and
Stella's lust for Stanley. The additional cuts remained
in place for over forty years, only being restored for
the 1993 theatrical re-release.

Although Vivien admired her director and
voiced her excitement at the collaboration, they
initially disagreed over how Blanche should be
portrayed on screen. According to her, Kazan was
"irritated" by Blanche. "I could not share his view
and I knew how it should be played after nine
months on the stage. I did it my way and Kazan
and I were finally in complete agreement." Kazan
saw it as more an issue of performance style. The
film version of *A Streetcar Named Desire* is significant for marking the moment in Hollywood history
when classical Hollywood came face to face with
method acting. Based on the ideas of Constantin

Stanislavski and taught by Lee Strasberg at the Actors Studio in New York, "the Method" was meant as opposition to the prewar mode of acting epitomized by stars such as Humphrey Bogart and Clark Gable. Students of the Method were encouraged to look within themselves and draw on raw emotions in order to add truth and depth to a character.

The entire Broadway cast—all Method actors—was transferred over for the film, with the exception of the Broadway Blanche, Jessica Tandy. Vivien was a much bigger name and Warner Bros. producer Charles K. Feldman wanted to ensure that *Streetcar* would be a financial as well as an artistic success. In the beginning, Kazan found the transition from Tandy to Vivien challenging. "When she came over here, she had the whole performance worked out, and it wasn't anything like what I like," Kazan said. "Larry's direction was an Englishman's idea of the American South—seen from a distance—and Vivien's conception of the role was a bit of a stereotype, just as my direction of a British character might be. . . . So for the first couple of weeks I had a lot of problems." Vivien's previous films prove that she had a more natural presence in front of the camera than many of her Hollywood peers, but in this instance she had difficulty separating from Olivier's direction and allowing Kazan to take over.

Although Olivier was busy immersing himself in the role of George Hurstwood for *Carrie*, there was a general suspicion on the set of *Streetcar* that the actor was counteracting Kazan's direction by coaching Vivien at home. Physically, Vivien went to lengths to transform herself into Blanche. *Silver Screen* noted, "She doesn't care how she looks, even welcoming the disfiguring lines and wrinkles which are artificially applied. She doesn't *want* to look beautiful. She doesn't care about favorable camera angles. She wants to be *Blanche*." Looking back on the film ten years later, Vivien said:

"Actual beauty—beauty of feature is not what matters, it's beauty of spirit and beauty of imagination and beauty of mind. I tried in *Streetcar* to let people see what Blanche was like when she was in love with her young husband when she was seventeen or eighteen. That was awfully important, because . . . you should have been able to see what she was like, and how this gradually had happened to her . . . you have to evoke this whole creature when she was young and when she was tender and trusting, as opposed to what she had become—cynical and hard, mad, and distressed and distraught."

Kazan wanted Vivien's transformation to be internal, as well as external. In the director's opinion, she "had a small talent, but the greatest determination to excel of any actress I've ever known. She'd have crawled over broken glass if she thought it would help her performance." It was not enough to play it safe and construct her character from the outside in, as Olivier was prone to do. To fully integrate with the rest of the cast, Vivien would have to dig deeper. Tapping into a well of emotions that she had yet to fully acknowledge was a daunting task. Once the floodgates opened, Vivien lost herself in the role and had difficulty shaking it off once filming ended. "I had nine months in the theater of Blanche DuBois," she told the *Los Angeles Times*. "Now she's in command of me in Hollywood."

On the whole, Vivien enjoyed working on *Streetcar*, noting that the process of making films seemed to have become more efficient during her absence from Hollywood. Kazan's directorial techniques were unlike anything she had experienced before. He sectioned off a space to use as a rehearsal hall where the cast would go over upcoming scenes while the sets were being prepared. It was his way of helping to "break in Vivien to a whole group of actors who had been working together for a long time."

Vivien appreciated her costars' effort to make her feel welcome. She particularly liked Kim Hunter, who played Stella. Hunter, in turn, praised Vivien's ability to read the script once and pinpoint exactly what needed to happen in order to make a scene work. Her *Gone With the Wind* costars had

LEFT: Vivien visits Olivier on the set of William Wyler's
Carrie at Paramount, 1950.

ABOVE: Vivien largely enjoyed working on *Streetcar*. Both
Marlon Brando and Kim Hunter praised her performance

Vivien's performance as Blanche was so
that the press called for the Academy of
Pictures to "Polish up an Oscar." She's p
in the harrowing final scene.

Vivien and Karl Malden in a crucial scene where Blanche
reveals the troubles of her past.

noticed this as well. It was a unique trait for a Hollywood actress to possess. "I had no sense of it
being extremely personal, the character of
Blanche," Hunter said in 1990. She thought Vivien
"a very determined person and a strong person in
many respects. The fact that I was totally unaware
of illness during the film says something."

Marlon Brando had a different view, although
he seemed to be examining the entire scope of
Vivien's life. In retrospect, he believed that Vivien
had been perfectly cast as Blanche because she
lived her character. "In many ways she *was*
Blanche," he wrote in his autobiography. "She was
memorably beautiful, one of the great beauties of

the screen, but she was also vulnerable, and her
own life had been very much like that of Tennessee's wounded butterfly. It paralleled Blanche's
in several ways, especially when her mind began to
wobble and her sense of self became vague."

Journalists who hoped for an explosive confrontation between England's reigning acting
queen and Hollywood's newest bad boy were in
for a disappointment. Vivien and Brando first met
in the Green Room on the Warner lot. They chat-

ted idly about their stage work before Brando joined Feldman and Kazan, leaving Vivien to finish her lunch. *Streetcar* was only Brando's second film and Vivien thought him at first "strange" and "terribly affected." He would ask her, "Why do you have to say good morning to everyone?" to which she'd reply, "Because it is a good morning and anyway it is a nice thing to say, so why not?" They became friendlier as filming progressed. Vivien was delighted to learn that her costar could "speak excellent English without a mumble" when he wanted to. Brando also impressed her with his talent for mimicry, often impersonating Olivier's speeches from *Henry V*. "He is the only man I

Karl Malden was the only cast member who thought Jessica Tandy had been better suited for Blanche. He disagreed with the sexuality Vivien evoked in the role.

have ever met who can imitate Larry accurately," Vivien said. "I closed my eyes and it could have been Larry."

The only cast member who never cottoned to Vivien's talent or charm was Karl Malden, who played Mitch in the film. He disagreed with the way Vivien accentuated the carnal undertones of Williams's play in her interpretation of Blanche, instead preferring Jessica Tandy's matronly portrayal. Malden's opinion of Vivien may have been colored by an incident that occurred off set. After filming ended, the Oliviers threw a party at Charles Feldman's house and invited everyone in the *Streetcar* cast. The Maldens arrived late to find that the other guests had already taken their seats for lunch. Malden was called over to a table and his wife Mona "finally ended up sitting on a swing by the pool all by herself." In his autobiography, Malden described how Vivien and John Buckmaster, who was visiting Hollywood, joined Mona on the swing. She and Buckmaster then proceeded to have a conversation with one another without acknowledging Mona. Malden took offense when Mona related the story to him afterward. "Vivien didn't need to be polite or even civil," he wrote, "after all, she was Scarlett O'Hara."

Much to Vivien's dismay, her Blanche inevitably drew comparisons to Scarlett. In 1958, when she appeared on Edward R. Murrow's television chat show *Small World*, Kenneth Tynan asked why she always found herself playing Southern belle roles. Vivien responded with, "Only twice, you know. Twice in oh, how many years? Twenty? So that's not many." She saw Blanche and Scarlett as "entirely different people" who had both been "knocked around," by circumstance "but one overcame the knocking around and the other succumbed." Vivien knew of the enormous success that *Gone*

Vivien was the only non-Method actor in *A Streetcar Named Desire*. She was also the only principal cast member who did not appear in the Broadway version. Pictured (L-R): Rudy Bond, Vivien, Kim Hunter, Nick Dennis, Marlon Brando.

With the Wind continued to enjoy, but perhaps because she had made a point to distance herself from both Hollywood and Scarlett, she was unaware of the firm grip the film had over the collective American consciousness. In the 1950s, there was a nostalgic fascination with the grandeur of upper-class life in the Old South, which both Scarlett and Blanche represented. By playing both these characters so successfully on film, Vivien became the cinematic archetype of the Southern belle; an image that still holds true today.

Elia Kazan thought Vivien excelled in the important scenes, and "was a hell of a lot better in the second half than she was in the first." Critics, however, were hard pressed to find any faults with her performance. With Blanche DuBois there emerged a new Vivien: a more mature actress capable of transmitting great depth and pathos. In Hollywood, she was "England's great Vivien Leigh," who possessed a "fluently expressive face, a pair of eyes that can flood with emotion and a body that moves with spirit and style." Richard Griffith of the *Los Angeles Times* thought she gave a "complete, devastating performance," and Bosley Crowther, who would present her with the New York Film Critics Circle award for Best Actress, had seldom seen "inner torments . . . projected with such sensitivity and clarity on the screen." *Holiday* magazine called for the Academy of Motion Pictures to "Polish up an Oscar . . . Vivien Leigh, as Blanche, plays the part with a perfection that cannot be pinned down in words." Vivien even managed to impress hard-boiled British critics. "One would have to be blind not to appreciate the brilliance of Vivien Leigh's performance," wrote C. A. Lejeune, who had been dismissive of some of Vivien's post-

Gone With the Wind film roles because she represented Hollywood rather than ideas of British national identity. "It is possible not to be touched by her, inconceivable not to be impressed and dazzled. Her Blanche is a woman shimmering in a sheath of gold, never very clearly seen, but taking glint and radiance from every facet."

In the following decades, there has been a critical tendency to favor the stark realism of Marlon Brando's groundbreaking performance. The melodramatic theatricality Vivien used for Blanche has been seen by some as a hindrance, a sign that her acting skills were rendered obsolete by the mumbling, brute force of Brando. In *The New Biographical Dictionary of Film*, David Thomson accused Vivien of seeming to be in an entirely different film than her costar. Knowing her theatrical background, it is deceptively easy to dismiss Vivien by saying that she plays style over substance. But such was the nature of her character. Blanche DuBois is an outmoded outsider who finds herself in a harsh modern environment, devoid of beauty and love, in which she has no place, and with which she is unable to cope.

"I've read Stanislavsky, naturally," Vivien said in 1960, "and it seems to me that the Method is: if you say something, you've got to mean it, and you've got to say it as interestingly as possible. But that applies to life—and acting is life, to me, and should be." On screen, Vivien was an equal match for Brando, and it was she who received the accolades during the 1952 awards season.

CHAPTER 6

BETWEEN THE DEVIL AND THE DEEP BLUE SEA

"[Vivien] was beautiful; she was spirited; she was, she kept reminding us, a Scorpio, and Scorpios get what they want, use it up, burn it up, leave nothing but golden memories and ash."

—Alec Guinness

Arriving home from Hollywood, the Oliviers immediately dove into plans for the 1951 Festival of Britain. The idea to present a double bill of Shaw's *Caesar and Cleopatra* and Shakespeare's *Antony and Cleopatra* on alternate nights had been suggested by set designer Roger Furse. It was an ambitious undertaking. While he was fully

---

Vivien as Shaw's Cleopatra. Photo by Angus McBean, 1951.

confident that Vivien would excel as Shaw's kittenish young queen, Olivier had initial reservations about her ability to tackle Shakespeare. Vivien admitted to sharing these feelings. She had scored critical successes with Jean Anouilh and Tennessee Williams but Shakespeare's great tragedies were considered the ultimate test in classical British theater, and the critics would be watching her like hawks to see how well she matched up with the heavyweight talent of her husband. Playing Ophe-

lia for a week in 1937 hardly counted toward what she would be expected to achieve now. It was a play she and Olivier hadn't planned to do for another ten years. Was she ready to grapple with the emotional maturity and technical expertise demanded by the part?

One of Vivien's greatest qualities as a performer was her determination to succeed where others seemed sure of her failure. "I have always tried to tackle things that I thought were beyond me," she said. With Olivier's help, she had completely transformed herself for *A Streetcar Named Desire*. This time, she needed little assistance. "She was brilliant," Olivier confessed in *On Acting*, "and in my opinion the best Cleopatra ever. She was radiant and beautiful and shone through the lines as if they had been written specially with her in mind. . . . She knew how to play the part. She seized it, fashioned and formed it, then showed us the magic." Critics on both sides of the Atlantic agreed. "A LASS UNPARALLEL'D" was the headline that greeted readers of *The Observer*. The London *Times* found her performance "faultless." In New York, Bosley Crowther hailed her as "superb." The critical and popular success of the two Cleopatras officially solidified the Oliviers's legendary status as the King and Queen of the British Stage. As Olivier recalled, "Vivien and I were set in the galaxy, and

LEFT: Arriving in Tilbury in December 1950, the Oliviers immediately began planning for the 1951 Festival of Britain.

TOP RIGHT: The Oliviers sail from New York on the French liner *Wyoming* after filming *Streetcar* and *Carrie* in Hollywood, November 1950.

RIGHT: Vivien pictured on the cover of *Festival* magazine in 1951.

fortunately everyone wanted to see us." Following a successful season at the St. James's Theatre in King Street, the production was transferred to New York, where Vivien and Olivier became the toast of Broadway. Playing to sold-out audiences at the famous Ziegfeld Theatre, they were caught up in a powerful whirlwind of celebrity.

On the night of March 20, 1952 Vivien sat in her dressing room listening to the twenty-fourth annual Academy Awards being broadcast live over the airwaves from the RKO Pantages Theatre in Hollywood. With twelve nominations, *A Streetcar Named Desire* was the frontrunner in many categories and Katharine Hepburn (nominated for *The African Queen*), was Vivien's only real competition for Best Actress. After hours of waiting, Ronald Colman's voice came over the radio and announced Vivien the winner for her powerful and emotionally charged performance. Press photographers were on hand to capture her reaction and the congratulatory kiss from Olivier. Unable to attend the show in person, Greer Garson accepted the award on Vivien's behalf. It was later presented to her during a special ceremony in London. The Oscar was the crowning achievement on an already glorious professional period for Vivien. She was the highest paid entertainer in Britain and was finally being

TOP LEFT: The Oliviers pictured at home in London with their Siamese cat New Boy, 1951. By now, they were considered the most popular show–business couple in Britain.

LEFT: The Oliviers, in costume for Shaw's *Caesar and Cleopatra*, share a tender moment backstage at the St. James's Theatre in London, 1951.

RIGHT: Publicity portrait of the Oliviers in *Caesar and Cleopatra*, 1951.

recognized as a thespian of real distinction rather than just a film star acting on stage. By all accounts this should have been a joyous time, but Vivien was unable to fully enjoy the fruits of her success. Behind the glittering and smiling social persona, she was drowning in the black depths of depression.

It would not be surprising if Kenneth Tynan factored into Vivien's forlorn mood. The Oxford-educated, illegitimate son of a Birmingham salesman was quickly gaining a reputation in London as a rising young critic who wielded a pen dipped in acid. He was, as American broadcaster Edward R. Murrow said, "if not angry, at least opinionated." Tynan had criticized several of Vivien's performances as far back as *That Hamilton Woman* (both she and Olivier were "terrible"). Of her Blanche DuBois in 1949, he described her as "a posturing butterfly, with no depth, no sorrow, no room for development, and above all, no trace of Blanche's crushed ideals." If the Oliviers or their fans had taken any notice of Tynan before, his opinion had been easily dismissed. Over the next decade, however, he would become a constant and distressing presence, adopting a personal vendetta against Vivien that was fueled by his flamboyant hero-worship for her husband.

Tynan relished attention and asserted his polarizing brilliance by stirring up controversy. Just as the Oliviers were receiving laurels for the two *Cleopatra* plays, Tynan was hired by *Evening Standard* editor Percy Elland first to take down comedian and singer Danny Kaye, who was all the rage

Angus McBean captured Vivien and Olivier in Shakespeare's *Antony and Cleopatra*, 1951. In his book *On Acting*, Olivier praised Vivien's performance, saying it was as if Shakespeare looked into the future and was inspired by Vivien.

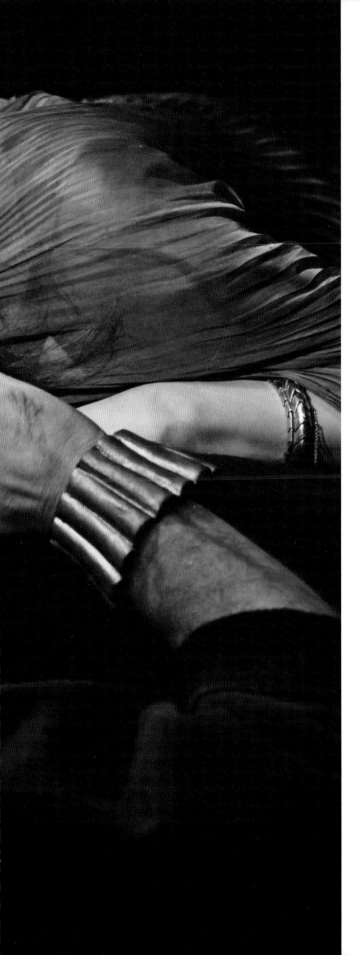

in London at the moment, and then to "put Vivien Leigh into her proper perspective." He readily stepped up to the challenge, taking aim at an aspect of Vivien's life to which she was becoming increasingly sensitive: her age. "Overpraise, in the end, is the most damaging kind of praise," Tynan wrote, "especially if you are an actress, approaching forty, who has already reached the height of her powers . . ."

It was a complete turn-around for a paper that, only six years earlier, had named Vivien "the only young actress on the English stage who is a star in her own right." Following a huge wave of backlash from readers, Tynan stepped down from his post at the *Standard* and took up residence at the more prestigious *Observer*, where he became the reigning advocate of counterculture in the British theater. The public never wavered in their support for Vivien; she had always been a people's actress. But her desire to stay on par with Olivier made critical opinions difficult to ignore, and Tynan's caused the most damage.

Staying in Gertrude Lawrence's luxurious apartment for the duration of their time in New York, Olivier reported coming home on several occasions to find Vivien sitting on the corner of their bed, wringing her hands and sobbing uncontrollably. His attempts at both comforting her and uncovering the reasons behind her distress proved useless. She also became abnormally obsessed with their social reputation. "Should we be too tired to go to a party, she would plow through every New York newspaper the next morning to see if our absence had been noticed." Olivier wasn't the only person in the company to witness Vivien's emotional fragility. Character actor

Wilfrid Hyde-White, who played Brittanus in *Caesar and Cleopatra*, remembered that she was "so ill that she would be shivering with weakness while waiting for her cue." It was a testament to her rigorous self-discipline and professionalism that she was able to shake off her symptoms during her performances. But when the curtain fell and her mood failed to stabilize, Olivier made the decision to seek psychiatric help.

"Actors are shy people and I swing between great happiness and misery," Vivien told journalist David Lewin in one of the few interview quotes that hinted at her struggle with manic depression. The subject was taboo in the mid-twentieth century, resulting in extreme ignorance and stigma from the public at large. For Vivien, outright public admission would have meant social ostracism and pro-

fessional suicide; she was willing to risk neither. But along with fear, she also felt a profound sense of shame at the unrecognizable person she became during periods of mania. An official verdict came in 1953, but due to her at-first-abnormal symptoms, she was variously diagnosed in New York with schizophrenia and hysteria. Terrified of what American doctors would reveal about her troubled psyche, she refused any suggestion of further consultations.

Sailing home to England a month later, Olivier arranged for them to stop over for a brief holiday in Jamaica. He hoped the sun and sea would be a tonic for Vivien, who was in dire need of rest. Staying at Noël Coward's Blue Harbour, Olivier disclosed his anxiety about Vivien to their long-time friend. Coward recounted his separate conversations with the couple in his diary: "Larry is worried about Vivien, who is having a sort of suppressed nervous breakdown. Had a long talk with her and tried to convince her that nervous exhaustion is the result of physical exhaustion, and that she needs a long rest. I can't bear to think of her being unhappy inside." When they left two days later, Coward recorded his own sense of worry about Vivien's mental stability. The fog of her depression was beginning to lift, but a storm was brewing on the horizon.

Vivien's choice for her next project sent up a red warning flag for her husband. *Elephant Walk*, based on the novel by Robert Standish, is the story of Ruth Wiley, a British woman who marries a tea

TOP LEFT: Vivien, in costume for *Antony and Cleopatra*, listens to the radio in her dressing room at the Ziegfeld Theatre in New York as the winners of the 1952 Academy Awards are announced.

TOP RIGHT: An expression of victory as her name is read out for the Best Actress award.

RIGHT: A congratulatory kiss from Olivier after Vivien won her second Academy Award.

planter and moves to his plantation in exotic British Ceylon. Her idyllic new life becomes complicated by her cultural isolation, attraction to the plantation overseer (Dana Andrews), a cholera epidemic, and an elephant stampede. Although *Elephant Walk* is typical of the action/adventure fare produced by Hollywood in the early 1950s, the roles lacked the normal standard of quality that both Vivien and Olivier consistently prided themselves in choosing to help further their careers. When Olivier declined the offer to play Vivien's leading man in order to finish post-production work on Peter Brook's *The Beggar's Opera*, which he was also producing, she cheerfully announced that her costar would instead be Peter Finch. For Olivier, the proverbial penny had dropped "with the knell of a high-pitched chapel bell."

The Oliviers discovered Finch on their Old Vic tour in 1948. Impressed by his performance in an unconventional production of *The Imaginary Invalid* staged on the floor of O'Brien's Glass Factory in Sydney, Olivier offered to take the young actor under his wing as a protégé. Encouraged, Finch moved to London with his wife, Ballets Russes dancer Tamara Tchinarova, and daughter Anita in 1949. His long-term contract with Laurence Olivier Productions allowed him to maintain relatively close contact with Britain's most famous acting couple. Finch had a reputation for being a hard-drinking hell raiser of the same caliber as Richard Burton and Peter O'Toole and Vivien found his unconventional good looks and rugged sexual-

TOP: Vivien accepts her Oscar for *Streetcar* in a special ceremony in London, June 1952.

LEFT: Vivien and Noël Coward attend the London premiere of Charles Chaplin's film *Limelight*, October 1952.

ity invigorating. On location in Ceylon, off the coast of her native India, the humid, nostalgic atmosphere exacerbated her already heightened mood and it wasn't long before she and Finch became entangled in an intense love affair.

Vivien's behavior during this period began to form a noticeable pattern that gradually settled into the classical rhythm of manic depression. Her moods cyclically alternated between crushing despair and abnormally high feelings of euphoria that, when left untreated, transformed into full-blown psychosis. She experienced these polarities of emotion on a grand scale that was largely misunderstood by those around her. It was almost like there were two Viviens in a near-constant state of warfare on the battlefield of her mind, and she was powerless to control it. Both phases overwhelmed and distorted her true nature to an extent that her loved ones found difficult to sympathize and cope with. At times, her depression lasted for more than a year. She became isolated within herself, lost confidence in her abilities as an artist, and found concentration difficult. Suicidal thoughts accompanied gut-wrenching anxiety. Sleeping became impossible without the aid of pills, and she lost weight because the anxiety made eating difficult. Depression made her feel "like a thing—an amoeba at the bottom of the sea." When the cyclone of mania struck it was sudden and powerful, and left in its wake a path of destruction that she was often unable to fully remember or repair. Within twenty-four hours, according to she would experience "marked elevation of mood and general activity. She rapidly loses her restraint and normal reserve, talks freely [with the press] . . . loses judgment, reasoning power and insight. In addi-

tion, she develops a marked increase in libido and indiscriminate sexual activity." In both phases, the high level of stress caused by her profession and hectic lifestyle was a major triggering factor.

Shortly after her arrival in Ceylon in late January 1953, Vivien began sending bizarre telegrams home to Olivier. She wrote of a sudden impulse to buy a horse, and of having a chat with a venomous snake that told her they should bring an acting company to the jungles of South Asia. Within two weeks, Olivier received an urgent request from Paramount producer Irving Asher. Vivien was disrupting production and was unable to remember her lines. It was unlike her normal, strictly professional attitude. Could Olivier *please* come to Ceylon immediately and talk some sense into her? Aware that he was coming to see her but most likely unaware as to the specific nature of his visit, Vivien sent off a cable saying it would be best if Olivier postponed his trip until the end of February and met her in Hollywood instead. Her suggestion was ignored.

Arriving in Colombo after a very long and exhausting journey, Olivier found Vivien waiting for him at the airport. In the car she insisted they stop off at a rest house for a drink and an intimate liaison, and flew into a rage when her husband rationally suggested they get her back to work. On the set in Kandy, Vivien's maid, Ethel Helmsing, filled Olivier in on the details. Vivien and Finch were both drinking heavily and she wasn't fit to do her job properly. On top of this she hadn't been sleeping, instead spending the nights with her costar on a hill under the stars. Four days later, realizing the only person who had any sort of influence over Vivien at the time was Finch, Olivier wished Asher

"all the luck he needed—which was a super-abundance of it . . ." and helplessly returned to England before seeking solace and advice from the composer Sir William Walton and his wife Susana at their home on the Italian island of Ischia.

Location shooting finished at the end of February, and the cast and crew of *Elephant Walk* left to complete the film on the Paramount backlot in Hollywood. Vivien's conduct continued to cause problems with the shooting schedule and lack of sleep was taking a physical and emotional toll. Despite a reminder from Olivier that she should ask for lighting tests, the Technicolor cameras relentlessly picked up on her fatigue. "I can't always be an ingénue," she snapped belligerently when this was pointed out. "I am 40 and if the movies don't like me, I'll stick with the stage where the make-up won't let them see my face. . . . Then people won't tell me I look tired and expect me to be a continual 19-year-old Scarlett O'Hara."

Perhaps ill advised, Vivien granted Hollywood gossip queen Louella Parsons an interview on the set. "I think this will be my last picture," she said offhand. "Life is too short to work so hard. I love Ceylon and want to go back in January and February. Come with me . . . you'll love it, and you should take time out and travel more. That's what I want to do next year, so I do not intend to make any more pictures." She then proceeded to call Parsons "vain" for sporting high-heeled shoes. Parsons noted her drawn look, nervous chatter and

---

1953: Vivien charms a cobra in Ceylon while filming William Dieterle's *Elephant Walk* (1954). The snake had been de-fanged.

fatigue, but "had no idea she was such a sick girl."

Off set, Vivien's relationship with Peter Finch had fizzled out for the time being. Given an ultimatum by his wife and possibly perturbed by the constant, demanding presence of his lover, Finch decided to make his exit. Not long after, word began to spread around the Hollywood film community that something sinister was afoot at Vivien's home. Her friend David Niven was asked to investigate. Driving to her rented mansion on Hanover Drive on the evening of March 11, Niven found a clearly deranged Vivien in the company of her former flame John Buckmaster, who Olivier described as being "barking mad" himself. Indeed, Gladys Cooper's son had recently spent time in a series of mental hospitals for his own mood disorder, and was the worst possible person to be around Vivien at a time when her mental capacity was colossally impaired. Buckmaster and Vivien had spent the evening carousing around the pool and they "enjoyed tearing up money, but she drew the line at his suggestion that they should fly out of an upper window together." Realizing he was ill-equipped to handle the two of them together, Niven enlisted the help of fellow British actor Stewart Granger. Together they managed to forcibly remove Buckmaster from the house and set out to try and subdue Vivien. It was a difficult and delicate task. Irving Asher needed to be informed that the star of his film was seriously ill and wouldn't be reporting to work in the morning, and Olivier had to be summoned from Europe. Both Niven and Granger were concerned that if the press learned that Vivien was experiencing a "crack up," she'd be finished in Hollywood.

The terrifying experience of looking after Vivien

Vivien with Peter Finch and Abraham Sofaer in *Elephant Walk*. Vivien and Finch began a torrid affair during filming.

during that weekend in 1953 was one that stuck with Niven and Granger for the rest of their lives. Decades later, they both recounted the incident in their respective memoirs (Niven used the pseudonym "Missie" to conceal Vivien's identity). Dr. Barney Kully was Vivien's physician in Hollywod. He called in a prescription of powerful sedatives for Granger to pick up at Schwab's Pharmacy and instructed Niven to lock away all knives and other sharp kitchen utensils. Kully then contacted psychiatrist Fraser McDonald. Vivien had been walking around nude save for a towel draped around her, and she was beginning to hallucinate. Niven man-

aged to coax her into watching television with him. At that hour of the night there were no programs on the air, but Vivien sat transfixed as the black and white screen buzzed and crackled. "Occasionally she would let out a peal of laughter and point at the set," Niven remembered. "Sometimes she would shrink back in horror; once she screamed with fear and moved up close beside me." Matters were made worse by her refusal to cooperate in taking the offered medication. Instead, she made Niven eat half of the drugged dinner Granger had cooked for her, causing him to pass out, and threw the remaining pills into the swimming pool. In the early hours of the morning, Dr. McDonald arrived with reinforcements.

Communication between Vivien and her husband had become less and less frequent in the days leading up to her breakdown. On March 6, she won a BAFTA for *Streetcar* and Olivier was at the Leicester Square Theatre to collect her statue. He lovingly cabled his congratulations, but expressed worry at not being able to talk to her by phone. In the past, the distance between them had always been filled by constant, arduous correspon-

dence. When Olivier finally reached Vivien's side, he was unprepared to deal with what awaited him. She was standing outside on the balcony; "her eyes were misted over, all grey-green-blue . . ." He described taking her in his arms, listening while she told him she was in love with Peter Finch (who was nowhere to be found), and learning of the crude treatment she'd been subjected to by Dr. McDonald's nurses.

Olivier and David Niven (center background) watch with worry as Vivien's blanket-covered body is put in the back of an ambulance in March 1953. She suffered a psychotic break in Hollywood while filming *Elephant Walk*. The *Los Angeles Times* reported that Olivier broke down and sobbed in Niven's arms.

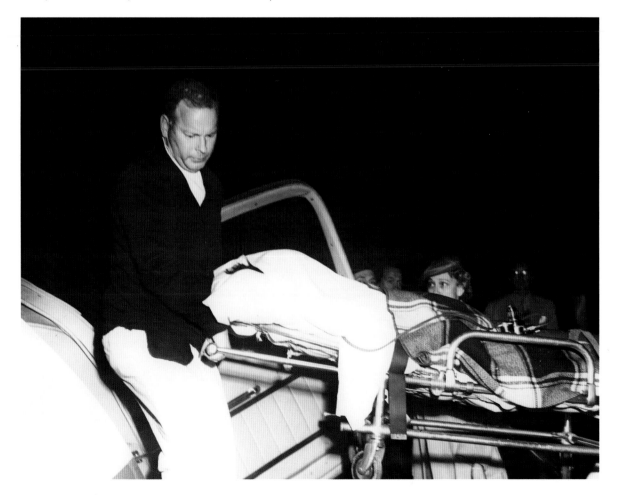

Vivien's first psychotic break happened at a time when the use of medication to treat severe mental illnesses was in its infancy. The first clinically tested antipsychotic had only been available since 1950 and the lack of drugs meant that many patients underwent experimental therapies that often did more harm than good and left them permanently scarred. In Hollywood, Vivien was given sodium injections and the "cold pack" to combat her aggression. She complained to Olivier of being strapped to her bed and wrapped in wet sheets, which her body temperature gradually warmed, sending her into a shocked, exhausted sleep. Gene Tierney, the Hollywood beauty famous for her roles in *Laura* and *Leave Her to Heaven*, underwent the

same procedure at a mental health clinic in Kansas, where she was also treated for manic depression. "When my time came, I felt only that I had been dehumanized," said Tierney. "To me the cold pack was the worst indignity of my confinement."

Bringing Vivien back to England was a purely financial decision. Even in the 1950s, private mental healthcare was enormously expensive. Paramount terminated her $175,000 contract—including living expenses—and replaced her with Elizabeth Taylor, although long shots of Vivien remain in the finished film. With no further paychecks coming from the studio, the cost of her treatment fell to Laurence Olivier Productions and the board decided they simply couldn't afford to let her stay in California. Instead, Olivier spent a total of fifty hours consulting with Dr. McDonald and his colleagues, Dr. Ralph Greenson and Dr. Martin Grotjahn, and arranged a room for Vivien at Netherne Hospital near Coulsdon, just south of London.

The long journey home was tiring for all involved. Despite efforts to prevent it, the international press caught wind of Vivien's crisis. Harrowing photographs of her blanket-covered body being loaded into the back of an ambulance while Olivier and David Niven anxiously supervised were splashed across the front pages. The *Los Angeles Times* reported that at the airport, the anguished actor broke down under the strain of the situation and sobbed in Niven's arms. In New York, Olivier and Danny Kaye had to restrain Vivien while she

After a long and difficult flight from New York, Vivien arrived in London with Olivier. Pictured behind them are her physician Armand Childe (left) and renowned psychiatrist Rudolf Freudenberg (right), who treated her at Netherne Hospital in Surrey. March 1953.

was sedated for the overseas flight. Terrified and angry, she violently resisted with all her might, "biting and scratching . . . screaming appalling abuse" at both men before finally succumbing to the tranquilizer that had been injected into her arm. The plane touched down in London in the late afternoon of March 20, 1953 amidst another barrage of photographers and curious bystanders. Vivien managed to smile for the crowd as she disembarked the aircraft with Olivier's assistance. That evening she became an involuntary inpatient at Netherne under the supervision of the renowned psychiatrist Dr. Rudolf Freudenberg. Olivier revealed the painful reverberation of Vivien's breakdown in an emo-

tional letter to his ex-wife, Jill Esmond:

"Getting her home was an incredible nightmare. As you may have gathered, she set up the strongest resistance, and of course as naturally follows when things go wrong, I was to her her worst enemy. She has suffered terribly and will be very ill for some time.

"But none of the horrors of the last ten days compare to the feeling of relief that somehow the mission was accomplished and that she is now safe in, I believe, the best hands in England. No one can see her for a bit so I am taking the time to recharge the batteries against whatever the future may hold . . ."

Nestled amongst the woodland and the country lanes of Hooley in Surrey, Netherne Hospital had been operating as a mental asylum since the Edwardian era. After the Second World War, it gained a worldwide reputation as a forward-thinking institution. During a visit in 1948, former First Lady Eleanor Roosevelt publicly declared that state mental asylums in America had a lot to learn from the work being done at Netherne. Dr. Freudenberg played a significant role in improving hospital conditions and pushed for widespread institutional reform as the Head of the Mental Health Section at the Ministry of Health.

A German-born psychiatrist who immigrated to Britain during the Nazi rise to power, Freudenberg had been a pioneer of insulin coma treatment for patients suffering from schizophrenia. As Physician Superintendent at Netherne, he set up a number

Vivien's first public appearance after her breakdown was at a party thrown by theatrical manager Binkie Beaumont in London, 1953.

of social programs for patients that included art therapy, occupational therapy, and social activities. He was described by his colleagues as "warm and humorous . . . a good teacher, a good listener, and a sympathetic friend to those in trouble." Olivier had been familiar with the doctor's work for some years. His older sister, Sybille, spent time as a patient at Netherne in 1948 and spoke of Freudenberg with admiration. Olivier appreciated his empathetic treatment toward Vivien.

Under Freudenberg's care, Vivien was put on a prolonged sleep regimen consisting of barbiturate-induced unconsciousness during which she received multiple doses of electroconvulsive therapy. In those days, ECT was widely used in the absence of advanced drugs to treat a multitude of psychiatric issues ranging from severe depression to obsessive-compulsive disorder. Administering the electric current while the patient was asleep was the preferable method because upon waking they usually didn't remember the treatment. The most common side effect was short-term memory loss but it was the actual experience of receiving ECT that caused the most discomfort and has since proved most controversial. Vivien's stepson Tarquin recalls seeing "burn marks on her temples where electrodes had been." During one course of treatment in 1955 she had a mild seizure afterward and walked out of Freudenberg's surgery with a large, swollen lip. In the years to come, Vivien would receive ECT on a voluntarily basis from several different psychiatrists, but was quick to cease treatment if she felt it wasn't administered successfully. However, in 1953 the combination of sleep and ECT seemed to help restore her to a semblance of her real self.

In Ischia, where he was again staying with the Waltons, Olivier was kept up to date about Vivien's progress at Netherne. The treatment was proceeding well, Freudenberg wrote on March 29, but her recovery would take time. She woke at four-hour intervals for meals and medicine, then went on sleeping. She often oscillated between cheerfulness and aggression, and recalled little of what had transpired since leaving Hollywood. This was to be expected. Despite Vivien's still-inconsistent moods, Freudenberg was hopeful about the outcome and was able to convince Vivien to stay on as a voluntary patient so that no extension of the legal order was necessary. On April 5, he found Vivien "quiet and friendly." He delivered one of Olivier's letters to her in the morning, and that evening she told him she "had received a very charming letter" from her husband.

Speculation about Vivien's illness seemed never-ending. Condolence letters came in from admirers as far away as India and Australia. Some suggested specialists and cures; more than one person advocated L. Ron Hubbard's new philosophy of Dianetics, practiced today by the Church of Scientology. But all of them made clear how loved Vivien was by her public. Alan Dent romanticized the situation by comparing her to a tragic French actress who died of tuberculosis at the height of her fame: "Well, dear, gracious, kind and beautiful creature, you have now had your warning. Your lamp had been turned too high, but it has been skillfully and in good time turned down by your devoted Larry. You have, to the world's relief, escaped the premature fate of the great Rachel [Elizabeth-Rachel Félix]."

For one young woman, Vivien's crisis changed

the course of her life. "Next Tuesday evening I am going to seek out a quiet corner and, at the age of 19, take stock of my life," her daughter Suzanne Holman was quoted as saying in the *Sunday Chronicle*. She was training at the Royal Academy of Dramatic Art at the time. "The misfortune that has come to my mother has made me ask myself this question: 'Shall I go on with my dream of becoming a great actress or should I be wiser to take up a career where there may be no triumphs, but where there would certainly be fewer heartaches and tears?'" In a 1950 interview for *Pictorial Review*, Vivien had mentioned trying to "discourage [Suzanne] from going on the stage."

Along with highlighting the challenges new actors face in trying to find work, Vivien also hinted at her own struggle to maintain her position at the top of her profession. Suzanne chose not to continue in her mother's footsteps, instead settling into a calm and quiet country life with her husband, insurance broker Robin Farrington, and their three sons.

After three weeks at Netherne, Vivien was discharged and transferred to University College Hospital in central London for further rehabilitative treatment. Friends and loved ones who poured in with gifts were relieved to find that the woman smiling back at them from the hospital bed was once again the same Vivien they all knew and adored. With enough rest and continued psychotherapy, she was assured a full recovery. To protect her from the prying eyes of the press, Olivier took her back to Notley, where they spent the spring restoring her to health and attempting to mend the rift in their relationship. The trauma of the past few months was not easily forgotten, and they both remained fearful of a recurring episode. According to Noël Coward, Vivien "solemnly promised to be good in the future, and not carry on like some mad adolescent of the twenties." But the demons, mania, and depression were constantly lurking in the shadows of her subconscious, and she would battle for the rest of her life to keep them at bay. Still, the prospect of returning to the work she so loved was something to look forward to. Terence Rattigan had written the star parts for her and Olivier in his new play, and by the end of summer, Vivien was again ready to take the stage.

Vivien circa 1953. Photo by Angus McBean.

CHAPTER 7

THE END OF THE AFFAIR

"There are only two things in my life which I am absolutely certain I would do over. The first is that I should become an actress—the second, that I should marry Laurence Olivier."

—Vivien Leigh, 1953

*T*he *Sleeping Prince* seemed the perfect play to usher Vivien back onto the stage after her illness. Terence Rattigan's "occasional fairytale" was originally planned to coincide with the coronation of Queen Elizabeth II in June 1953, but was postponed to give its star sufficient time to recover. That it opened four months behind schedule made

Vivien as Viola in Shakespeare's *Twelfth Night*, directed by John Gielgud at the Shakespeare Memorial Theatre in Stratford-upon-Avon, 1955. Photo by Angus McBean.

no difference to fans that clamored to see Vivien as Cinderella-like Mary Morgan, the American chorus girl who falls in love with a stuffy Carpathian duke (played by Olivier). The public was glad to see "all the old liveliness, all the old Leigh vivacity" shining brightly. Olivier thought the play trivial fun and praised Vivien for being "bewitching in the piece." After a charity show in Manchester that raised £12,000, *The Sleeping Prince* sold out in Glasgow, Edinburgh, Newcastle-upon-Tyne, and Brighton before heading to London, where it opened at the Phoenix Theatre on Vivien's fortieth birthday and

The Sleeping Prince was the perfect light comedy to welcome Vivien back onto the stage. The play opened at the Phoenix Theatre in London on November 5, 1953. Photos by Angus McBean.

ran until July 1954.

The Oliviers followed *The Sleeping Prince* with separate film projects for Alexander Korda. Olivier filmed Shakespeare's *Richard III*, with Claire Bloom taking over Vivien's role as Lady Anne. Vivien chose to star in a screen version of Rattigan's 1952 play *The Deep Blue Sea*, directed by Ukranian-born Anatole Litvak and filmed in CinemaScope.

In theory, *The Deep Blue Sea* was a recipe for success. With *The Winslow Boy* and *The Browning*

Version behind him, Rattigan was enjoying his popularity as one of England's greatest dramatists. "Tola" Litvak had been a widely respected director in Europe, heavily influencing Max Ophüls, before going to Hollywood. His most famous film prior to being contracted by Korda was the harrowing drama *The Snake Pit*, starring Olivia de Havilland as a patient in a mental hospital.

The prestigious combination of Rattigan and Litvak should have inspired memorable artistry. In practice, however, it was not a happy experience. Work seemed to have a stabilizing influence on Vivien, but the heavy subject matter of this latest

RIGHT AND NEXT PAGE: Vivien as American showgirl Mary Morgan in Terence Rattigan's *The Sleeping Prince*, 1953.

WEEK ENDING NOVEMBER 7 1953   EVERY WEDNESDAY FOURPENCE

ILLUSTRATED

Vivien Leigh's Striking New Rôle

SEE STORY INSIDE

Fabian's Crime Dossiers
ACTRESS AND THE KIDNAPPER

HUSH-HUSH TRANSFER OF ROYAL POWERS
Princess Margaret And The Regency

film could not have helped to elevate her mood. Rattigan's story covers a day in the life of modern-day Anna Karenina, Hester Collyer, the well-to-do wife of a prominent British judge who has left her sexually vacant but stable marriage after falling passionately in love with former RAF pilot Freddie Page. Hester sacrifices everything for Freddie, giving up her comfortable life to move into his dingy flat. Not long afterward, the relationship becomes one-sided and Hester's unrequited passion leaves her isolated and suicidal.

Despite his warm relationship with Vivien, Korda took a risk in casting her in *The Deep Blue Sea*. The *Elephant Walk* incident had made her largely uninsurable. Should she be unable to finish the film for any reason, a substantial investment would be lost. Yet, despite her recent troubles, Korda believed in Vivien's sustained power at the box office. He paid her a salary of £65,000 and gave her a final say in casting. The supporting players were comprised of some of British cinema's most interesting character actors, including Emlyn Williams as Sir William Collyer, and the delightfully sinister Eric Portman as Mr. Miller.

Vivien's approval of Kenneth More as her lover was the only peculiar choice. Physically, he was far removed from her typical leading men, but he was one of the most popular British stars of the moment and had played Freddie Page in the orig-

inal theatrical production. It turned out to be a casting mismatch. The air between them was frigid, and their onscreen chemistry awkward. They often argued on the set about characterization. According to More, Vivien "wanted glamour—and continuous praise for her beauty—in a script which basically depended upon a woman who had unattractive and tiresome sides to her." More disliked Vivien as an actress and as a person, and wasn't shy about saying so. When asked by Alan Dent to contribute to a compilation of memories following Vivien's death, the actor wrote that he "could never really trust her and I suspected her almost overwhelming friendliness. I thought she was petulant, spoilt, overpraised and overloved."

Jean Howard photographed Vivien and Anatole Litvak on location in Klosters, Switzerland for one of the film's flashback sequences. According to her,

---

RIGHT: The Oliviers circa 1954.

NEXT SPREAD LEFT: Vivien was beautiful as Terence Rattigan's tragic Hester Collyer, but much to her disappointment, a majority of critics thought she was miscast in *The Deep Blue Sea*.

NEXT SPREAD RIGHT: Vivien and Kenneth More on location in Klosters, Switzerland.

LEFT: Publicity portrait of Vivien for Anatole Litvak's *The Deep Blue Sea* (1955).

Litvak had a reputation "second only to George Cukor's as a woman's director." Given Vivien's close friendship with Cukor, it seems strange that she and Litvak didn't enjoy a similar relationship. In a 1955 interview with *Picturegoer*, Vivien said that Litvak was "a fine director. Very understanding and very patient." Moira Lister, who played Hester's nosy neighbor Dawn Maxwell, got a different impression. "He had this theory that you have to destroy somebody first to get a good performance out of them," Lister told Hugo Vickers, "and he used to—systemically—every day—destroy Vivien until he got her to cry, and he said, 'Right. Now you're in a mood to do the scene. We'll do the scene.' He was really very harsh with her."

While some critics such as the *New York World-Telegram*'s Alton Cook applauded Vivien for "one of her most brilliant achievements," the general opinion was that she had "seriously mis-cast herself" in the film. Her friend Alan Dent gave a brutally honest estimation of her performance: "No amount of sheer integrity could make Vivien credible in the part of Hester in which Peggy Ashcroft—and later on in the run, Googie Withers—had seemed so dead right in the original version.

LEFT: Anatole Litvak had a similar reputation to George Cukor as a woman's director, but he and Vivien did not enjoy a close relationship. Vivien is pictured with Olivier and George Cukor in Los Angeles, February 1957.

RIGHT: Vivien photographed by Angus McBean in 1956.

Vivien's beauty and elegance were against her from the start. . . . She did nothing—or was asked by her director to do nothing—to modify the impression she gave of a dazzling young woman of the world who would be extremely unlikely to ever find herself in Hester's predicament."

Vivien was disappointed with the reviews and later counted the film among the mistakes of her career. Michael Denison, who did a charming turn as Algernon Moncrieff in Anthony Asquith's *The Importance of Being Earnest*, saw *The Deep Blue Sea* when it was released to cinemas in August 1955. Contrary to many critics, he thought Vivien wonderful and told her so. "Tears came into her eyes and she said, 'Oh thank you Michael. . . . You know if you read what they've written about my performance in that film you would think I'm a

woman who has never experienced love or anything else.'"

It would be the last film Vivien made for Korda and was one of only two titles in her post-*Gone With the Wind* filmography that didn't turn a profit—the other being *Anna Karenina*, also distributed by Twentieth Century-Fox. Litvak's film has long-since disappeared from mainstream circulation. Sadly, it still failed to resurface with the release of Terence Davies's 2011 remake, starring Vivienesque actress Rachel Weisz as Hester.

In March 1955, the Oliviers traveled to Stratford-upon-Avon to headline a trio of Shakespeare's most famous plays for a repertory season at the Shakespeare Memorial Theatre. They were both at a pivotal point in their careers and this promised to be a stressful undertaking. "I'm never satisfied with my performances," Vivien admitted. "But I'm an actress. An actress should play anything she considers worthwhile. . . . When a good part comes along—comedy or drama—I take it." On offer were Viola in *Twelfth Night*, Lady Macbeth with Olivier in the title role, and the hapless Lavinia in the violent revenge play *Titus Andronicus*.

The highlight of the season was *Macbeth*, directed by Glen Byam Shaw. Today, this production is considered "one of the best *Macbeth*s, if not the best, of our time." Theater historian

Michael Mullen believed that being married to Olivier made Vivien "exceptionally convincing as Macbeth's wife. . . . In her sensual beauty there was ample explanation for Macbeth's fascination, and it implied a gain, not a loss, of manliness in his drive to fulfill her expectations." She lowered her voice to give her character more authority and made full use of "the great gestures that the role invites."

Vivien's Lady Macbeth was greatly appreciated by many critics and fellow actors. "Vivien Leigh is a revelation," wrote Alan Dent in the *News Chronicle*. The *Daily Mail*'s Cecil Wilson thought her "frail beauty" took on "a new steely strength." And the theater critic for *The Scotsman* said she "attains complete mastery of the part." Noël Coward thought her "quite remarkable" and "brilliant" in the banqueting scene. Olivier went further. In his

opinion, she was not merely good; she was the greatest Lady Macbeth he had ever seen. It was a sentiment he maintained throughout his life. When John Clements took over the directorship of the Chichester Festival Theatre in 1965, he asked Olivier which actress he should cast as Lady Macbeth. Olivier replied, "If you want the very best, get Vivien."

"I always used to worry so much when I acted with Larry in case I let him down," Vivien told David Lewin in 1960. "He is a genius you see, and I didn't think I could keep up with him and so it was a strain. I wanted more than anything else to film *Macbeth* with him but even before I played the part for the first time on stage I said to Larry, 'If you don't think I can do it, get someone else.'" It was this self-criticism and fear of failure that made Vivien ignore the praise she received—including Olivier's—and instead focus on one particularly negative review.

"Last Tuesday Sir Laurence shook hands with greatness," Kenneth Tynan wrote in the *Observer* on June 12, 1955. "Miss Vivien Leigh's Lady Macbeth," on the other hand, "is more niminy-piminy than thundery-blundery, more viper than anaconda, but still quite competent in its small way." The none-too-subtle implication that Vivien had no business being on the same stage as her husband was the straw that broke the camel's back. Tynan had been vitriolic toward Vivien for years but his reviews of the Stratford season took things to a new level. Olivier noted that her illness seemed to add fuel to the critical fire, with Tynan referring to her as "his stricken lady" in his review of *Twelfth*

The Oliviers attend the wedding of Vivien's daughter Suzanne to Robin Farrington, December 6, 1957.

Night. Tynan knew how hard Vivien pushed herself to mature as an artist and how seriously she took her craft. Still, he came at her like a hawk with talons out, intent on tearing her to pieces with his words. In a 1983 interview with Olivier, Tynan's widow Kathleen said that Tynan's attacks on Vivien in 1955 were "completely unnecessary." In the same interview, Olivier bluntly explained the situation: "To Ken, Vivien was an interloper between me and my fucking genius." Only posthumously did Vivien get the appraisal she deserved. Tynan recanted his opinion in the 1970s, calling his review of Vivien's Lady Macbeth one of the "worst errors of judgment he had ever made."

Noël Coward spent an evening at Notley after one performance of *Macbeth* and observed to his "true horror" that Vivien was headed for another breakdown. "She is obsessed, poor darling by the persecutions of the press." Olivier blamed Tynan but Coward saw a bigger picture. He believed the couple's acting partnership had become as problematic as their married life. Vivien needed to deviate from Olivier as far as her career was concerned. "She should develop along her own lines and become a witty, light comedienne, which she could do better than anyone I can think of…" Only then, in Coward's opinion, could she "achieve a position in which she is unassailable."

The crash came when they were rehearsing *Titus Andronicus,* the last play of the season. In his

TOP: The Oliviers by Angus McBean, circa 1957.

RIGHT: Olivier in the title role and Vivien as his daughter Lavinia in Shakespeare's *Titus Andronicus,* 1955. Photo by Angus McBean.

autobiography, Olivier wrote that when Vivien was manic, he felt responsible for her and was afraid to let her out of his sight. Her tendency to wander outside in the early morning was especially worrying. They were living at Avoncliffe, the company's house in Stratford. Vivien could drown in the river at the bottom of the garden or get hit by a car speeding down the road after one of her epic parties. She spent lavishly and slept little. At one point, Olivier convinced her to drive with him to Surrey to see Dr. Freudenberg at Netherne. Vivien agreed, but when they arrived she acted as if nothing was wrong and no treatment was required. It was part of the pattern. Olivier believed that Vivien made an effort to hide the problem from everyone except himself.

Vivien's manic energy took its toll on her performance in *Titus*. Her part was small compared to Olivier's, and her character Lavinia spends much of the play with her tongue cut out and her hands chopped off. Nevertheless, she was unable to fully concentrate, "as if she had lost touch with her craft." Olivier knew it was a symptom of her illness, but those less familiar with her situation simply thought the part too difficult for her. John Gielgud, who experienced difficulty directing the pair in *Twelfth Night* earlier in the season, attended a performance and found Vivien "in a very bad way. She is utterly ineffective on stage—like paper, only not so thick, no substance or power—and off stage she is haunted, avid, malicious and insatiable, a bad look-out for the future and poor Larry who is saint-like with her and play-acting most beautifully as well." Work was the most important thing to Olivier and he began sleeping in his dressing room at the theater or driving to Notley for the night.

ABOVE: *Macbeth* was the highlight of the 1955 Stratford season. It was thought by many that being married enhanced the Oliviers's understanding of the characters they played.

RIGHT: Vivien was the "very best" Lady Macbeth, in Olivier's opinion. Photo by Angus McBean.

Vivien stayed at Avoncliffe, where Peter Finch kept her company.

By early 1956, Vivien had largely recovered from her latest episode and accepted the leading role in Noël Coward's play *South Sea Bubble*, a modern dress comedy set on a tropical island in the South Pacific. She recounted an amusing story about the play to Coward biographer William Marchant. It began over lunch at The Ivy during the mid-1940s. Vivien was still recovering from TB and was desperate to get away to a warmer climate, but the postwar ban on foreign travel made things difficult. Inspired by Coward's recent musical, *Pacific 1860*, Vivien had it in mind to visit the island of Samolo, unaware that it was a fictional location.

Coward agreed to speak to Health Minister Aneurin Bevan on her behalf and then began to talk about a new play he wanted to write titled *Island Fling*. "I was so tired and rheumy that for the moment I didn't want to think about work or plays or anything of the kind," Vivien said, "and only with some persuasion did I manage to get him back on the subject of Samolo."

Pendarla was the place to stay, Coward told her, and he could make an introduction with the governor's wife, Lady Alexandra Shotter. He warned Vivien about a host of other interesting characters she was likely to encounter on the island, and told her about a villa she could rent. Vivien went back to Durham Cottage to begin her vacation plans, "ready to weep in anticipation." She didn't have a beach wardrobe in London but was looking forward to spending a week shopping for "cruise clothes" in New York while Olivier was performing there with the Old Vic. In the library, she pulled an old atlas off the shelf, but couldn't find Pendarla or the Samolan Islands. Geography had never been her best subject, however, so she "rang up the British Travel Association on an impulse, thinking perhaps they'd send me some literature." The travel agent "was very sympathetic but regretted to inform me that the island of Samolo was a figment of Noël Coward's imagination!"

Marchant remarked that Coward's joke seemed

LEFT: Vivien as Lady Alexandra Shotter in Noël Coward's *South Sea Bubble*, 1956.

TOP RIGHT: In 1956, Vivien met her teenage idol, Ramon Novarro.

BOTTOM RIGHT: With Olivier and Joan Crawford at a dinner party in London, 1956.

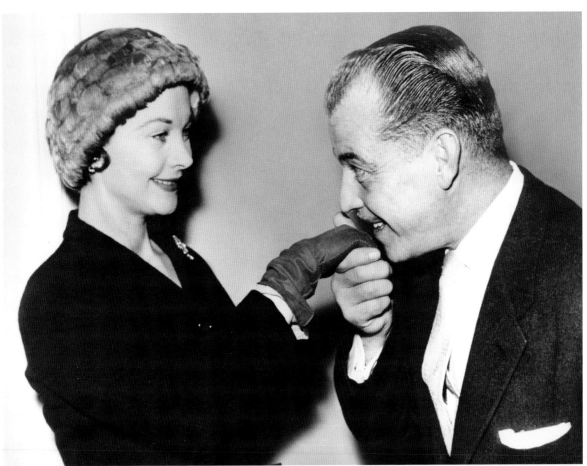

uncharacteristically mean-spirited, but Vivien's eyes crinkled in merriment as she explained to him that Coward had been telling her about his play the entire time. "When he talked about Lady Alexandra Shotter, the Governor's wife, that was the character he had in mind for me . . ."

South Sea Bubble completely booked out in advance, but Vivien wouldn't see the run to completion. On July 12, the Oliviers held a press conference at their new London home, Lowndes Cottage, to announce that they were expecting their first child just in time for Christmas. Vivien observed that at nineteen, she had been one of the youngest actress-mothers. Now, at forty-two, she would be one of the oldest. She had already hired a nanny and had chosen yellow and white as

the colors for the nursery at Notley Abbey. They hoped for a girl, who they would name Katherine. "Oh, you know men," she teased, looking up at Olivier who was standing behind her, "They like to be comforted in their old age with a daughter."

Noël Coward learned about the baby shortly before it became public knowledge. Vivien contacted him in Bermuda, where he was living as a tax exile, saying her doctor had advised she leave *South Sea Bubble* and rest. Olivier had planned to fly to Paris to tell Coward in person but was held up with work. Coward was angered not only by the fact that Vivien had known she was expecting since the beginning of his play's run, but because for years he had been the Oliviers's closest confidant when it came to matters of their personal lives. He

felt slighted, writing to Binkie Beaumont, "Although the dubious sanctity of the Oliviers's home means a great deal to me, the financial security of my own means a bloody sight more. . . . I do I do I do I do wish that the long awaited reunion of two minds had been a trifle less enthusiastic and a little more thoughtful of others." Coward also expressed private concern for the baby's welfare and predicted it would make an early appearance and surprise everyone. His words were prophetic. Vivien left the play on August 11 and miscarried the following day.

Hester St. John-Ives was married to Olivier's older brother Dickie and lived in the cottage at Notley Abbey since 1953. She was there when Vivien had the miscarriage and witnessed the heartache it caused. Hester isn't sure whether a baby would have saved the Oliviers's relationship, or provided the key to Vivien's happiness. Based on Vivien's track record with Suzanne, "she certainly wouldn't want a child to interfere with her own life." But reflecting on how Vivien treated her eldest daughter Louise when she was younger, Hester believes that Vivien "would have got a lot of fun out of being a mother again. She absolutely adored having a little creature to go around the garden with a miniature trowel with her."

The feeling that she was responsible for the stress Olivier endured while directing the notoriously difficult Marilyn Monroe in *The Prince and the Showgirl* compounded Vivien's grief. The casting had been her idea to begin with. While performing in *The Sleeping Prince* in 1953, Vivien saw *How to Marry a Millionaire* at the cinema and became fascinated by Marilyn. "I thought, heaven help me, that she was very funny. I said to Larry: 'This girl is wonderful in comedy,' and suggested Marilyn star in the film version." She added that she thought herself too old for the role. To her dismay, Olivier relished the idea and hoped that making a film with the Hollywood bombshell would be a new stimulus for his career. When Vivien changed her mind and suggested she might like to revive

FAR LEFT: Vivien sees Olivier off at the airport on a snowy morning in February 1956. Olivier flew to New York to meet with Marilyn Monroe for the upcoming film *The Prince and the Showgirl.*

LEFT: Vivien with Olivier, Marilyn Monroe, and Arthur Miller after the Millers arrived in London for *The Prince and the Showgirl,* July 1956.

RIGHT: Vivien and Olivier attend the premiere of *The Prince and the Showgirl* at the Warner Theatre, London. June 1957.

ABOVE LEFT: Vivien, in costume for *Titus Andronicus*, tells reporters about her plan to help save the beloved St. James's Theatre, 1957.

ABOVE RIGHT: Vivien leads a protest march down the Strand in July 1957. Joining her were Olivier (right) and several other members of the theatrical profession.

RIGHT: July 1957, Vivien stands outside the St. James's Theatre on King Street. Olivier had leased the theater in 1949 and she was determined to save it from demolition.

Mary Morgan on screen after all, Olivier and Terence Rattigan said: "Oh, but you're too old."

Olivier's opinions about Marilyn have been well documented on both page and screen. At first he was sure he would fall in love with her, but he quickly changed his mind once cameras started rolling. As the film was financed by Marilyn Monroe Productions, Olivier didn't have to worry about money but he did resent his time being wasted. Everything about Marilyn's work ethic clashed with his. Out of the fifty-three days it took to make the film, she only showed up on time for three and habitually forgot her lines. Marilyn was trained in the Method style but what annoyed Olivier was her insistence on having Lee Strasberg's wife, Paula, as her constant companion and pseudo-director on set. All together, Olivier and many of the cast and

The Oliviers participated in several charity events throughout their marriage, including the annual Night of a Hundred Stars at the London Palladium. The event was organized by Noël Coward to raise money for the Actors Orphanage. In 1956, Vivien, Olivier, and John Mills performed a song and dance routine to Irving Berlin's "Top Hat, White Tie and Tails." The trio is pictured with Hollywood star Tyrone Power, who sang "Chattanooga Choo Choo."

crew thought Marilyn unintelligent, untalented, and unprofessional. She had undeniable star quality but was, in Olivier's words, "a model, not an actress." Nearly thirty years would pass before Olivier could look back on the film and acknowledge his "tetchy" attitude and Marilyn's "star performance."

It is not impossible to think that Vivien and Mar-

ABOVE: The Oliviers feeding the pigeons in Piazza San Marco, Venice, during the 1957 European tour of *Titus Andronicus*.

ABOVE AND BELOW LEFT: In Venice for the 1957 *Titus Andronicus* tour.

BELOW: With Olivier in Paris for the *Titus Andronicus* tour, 1957.

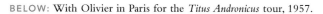

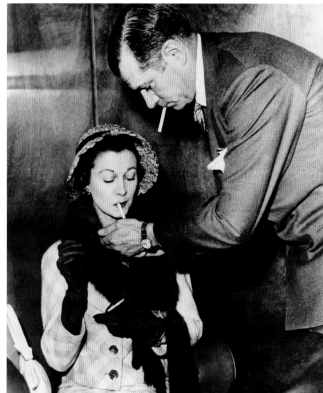

ilyn might have formed a kinship had they gotten to know one another better. Marilyn lacked Vivien's stature as an actress and a respected celebrity, but they had much in common on a personal level. Like Vivien, Marilyn had her demons (according to biographer Adam Victor, modern-day psychiatrists believe Marilyn suffered from borderline personality disorder. She later spent time in a mental institution). But despite their troubles, they both had a vulnerability that endeared them to many people. Vivien had been the only non-American and non-Method actor in *Streetcar Named Desire*. She knew what it was like to be an outsider on a film set, as Marilyn had been on *The Prince and the Showgirl*, and to lack confidence in her own abilities as an actress. Both strived to avoid typecasting and to prove themselves as something more than

Vivien and Olivier on an amusement ride at Battersea Festival Gardens during a lavish party thrown by Elizabeth Taylor's husband, producer Mike Todd, July 2, 1957. Todd had offered to finance Olivier's *Macbeth* film, but his tragic death in March 1958 caused the film to be shelved indefinitely.

just a pretty face or a sex symbol. As it was though, Vivien sided with Olivier and she and Marilyn remained rivals at best.

Not long after *The Prince and the Showgirl* wrapped, Olivier began rehearsing what would become one of his greatest characters: the seedy music hall performer Archie Rice in John Osborne's *The Entertainer*. Vivien could not have foreseen the rift that lay ahead when she took Olivier to see *Look Back in Anger* at the Royal Court in Sloane

Square the previous spring. Osborne's debut play ushered in the era of the kitchen sink drama and suddenly the landscape of British theater began to change. The escapist plays of Noël Coward, and Terence Rattigan—in which Vivien had made her name—were being replaced by gritty social realism that focused on the plight of the middle class. Olivier didn't think much of *Look Back in Anger* upon first viewing. After seeing it again with Arthur Miller, he decided this was the direction his career needed to move in and asked Osborne to pen a new play for him.

Vivien correctly suspected that Olivier was using *The Entertainer* to drive a wedge into their marriage. Since 1948 Olivier had actively looked for plays that suited them as a couple. He chose Dorothy Tutin to play his daughter and suggested

Vivien meets with Felix Fenston, the developer who purchased and planned to demolish the St. James's Theatre to make way for a block of offices.

that Vivien could play Archie's wife; she was too young and beautiful, he knew, but perhaps this could be disguised with a rubber mask. Osborne and director Tony Richardson quickly dismissed the idea: "The British public would never accept her as aging, ugly and common." Osborne liked Vivien and sensed what was happening between her and Olivier. He felt it important to engage her support, inviting her to accompany him and Olivier to London's few remaining music halls for research and allowing her to sit in on rehearsals at the Royal Court. Vivien had always been perceptive and good at reading people. Olivier would adapt to his surroundings, but there was no place for her in this new theatrical movement. The style was shifting from her corner, and Olivier was shifting with it.

"None of us likes to admit defeat, and I think this may be especially true of the members of the theatrical profession. With us optimism must be an essential ingredient of our lives." Vivien wrote this for the foreword to W. Macqueen-Pope's memorial book *St. James's: Theatre of Distinction*. It was as much a statement about her life as it was about a piece of London's theater history disappearing. She had a sentimental attachment to the building, not least because she had played there many times throughout her career. When Olivier leased the St. James's in 1949 it became the symbol of their reign as theater royalty. Now, like their marriage, the St. James's was under threat and Vivien became

determined to save it from demolition.

Vivien's crusade made headlines from the start. On July 11, 1957 she interrupted a debate in the House of Lords and was forcibly escorted from the building. It was an admittedly impulsive move, but she felt provoked by one member of Parliament's comment that the 122-year-old St. James's was "simply an obsolete, Victorian, inconvenient, uncomfortable playhouse with no architectural or historic value." She then led a large group of theatrical colleagues down the Strand carrying banners and sandwich boards. This was followed by an appearance on television with Felix Fenston, the developer whose company had purchased the theater.

The press wrote of Vivien's demonstration in a chastising tone. In private, her new psychiatrist Arthur Conachy labeled her adoption of the cause a symptom of mania. To the public, however, she became a kind of hero. People were overjoyed that a figure of Vivien's stature would be so vocal about wanting to preserve their national heritage. Letters poured in from as far afield as Scotland thanking her for her "brave," "gallant," "admirable," and "moving" protest. She was compared to a suffragette and hailed as someone with good sense and courage. One woman from Hampstead said that if only there were more women like Vivien, "England would be all the better for it."

Despite Vivien's efforts, it was impossible to raise enough money to buy the theater out of the developer's hands. The St. James's closed on July

Despite the presence of their daughter Suzanne, Vivien was chastised by the press for vacationing with her ex-husband Leigh Holman in Italy in 1957. The holiday fueled rumors of an impending breakup between her and Laurence Olivier.

20, 1957 and was razed in October to make way for a block of offices. "She failed, but she failed gloriously, because the odds against her were too heavy," wrote W. Macqueen-Pope, affectionately. "But we English always love a loser. And those of us who loved the St. James's will cherish the thought of Miss Leigh for her splendid fight to aid something in which we believe." Today, a Theatre-land plaque at the site of the former St James's commemorates Vivien's "epic campaign."

The disintegration of the Oliviers's marriage was a gradual and painful process. Noël Coward observed that they were "trapped by public acclaim, scrabbling about in the cold ashes of a physical passion that burnt itself out years ago . . . They are eminent, successful, envied, and adored, and most wretchedly unhappy." At the heart of the matter was Olivier's inability to cope with Vivien's illness. She did not yet willingly seek treatment for her episodes and it wasn't until 1959 that she con-fronted the fact that what she suffered from was more than "bits of exhaustion, etc., or nervous-ness." By that time, however, Olivier had already made up his mind to leave.

Before taking on the St. James's campaign, the Oliviers toured Europe with *Titus Andronicus*. It was a pre-agreed extension of the 1955 Stratford season. While the play was successful, the tour was an emotional disaster for Vivien. Stories abound of sleepless nights, cursing on stage, heavy drinking, broken windows on trains, and terrorizing other cast members. There was even a story told by

Olivier's assistant Colin Clark about Vivien punch-ing a policeman in Yugoslavia. Upon their return, the play was transferred to the Stoll Theatre in Lon-don for a short season. The party that followed has gone down in history as one of Vivien's most extravagant. Hester and Dickie were in attendance at Notley and Hester remembers, "People were passed out on the front lawn and Lady Diana Cooper was in chain mail. We made the gazpacho in Louise's baby bath." The board members of the Shakespeare Memorial Theatre weren't amused to receive a bill for thousands of pounds.

A few months later, Vivien confronted Olivier about rumors that he wanted to marry the much younger actress Dorothy Tutin. What followed was cited by Olivier as the catalyst for his decision to leave their marriage. As Olivier wrote it, he had just gone to sleep on the night of July 31 when Vivien

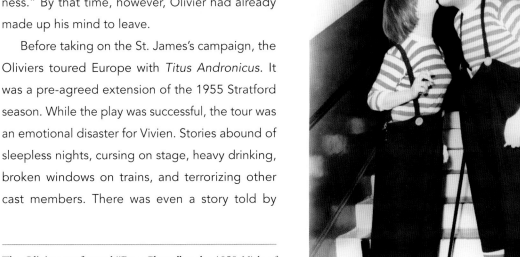

The Oliviers performed "Be a Clown" at the 1958 *Night of a Hundred Stars*.

began whipping him across the face with a wet washcloth. When he locked himself in another room, Vivien followed and relentlessly pounded on the door. Olivier eventually snapped, opened the door, grabbed Vivien by the wrist and threw her across her bedroom. He meant to throw her on the bed but she caught the corner of her eye on the nightstand. The next day they made an appearance at the Housing Ministry as part of the St James's protest. Vivien wore a black eye patch and told reporters it covered an insect bite. In reality, the situation was much more serious. She could have been killed.

The Oliviers still appeared in public together on occasion but keeping up appearances was difficult. When they took separate vacations in August 1957, the press suspected that something was amiss. Vivien traveled to Italy with Leigh Holman and Suzanne while Olivier went to Scotland with Tarquin to scout locations for *Macbeth*. The film had been in the planning stages since 1955 and Vivien longed for the chance to play Lady Macbeth on screen. Olivier had even written a script but the funding was difficult to come by. Alexander Korda had offered but died suddenly of a heart attack in 1956. Several other financial opportunities had fallen through, as

LEFT: Vivien kisses Olivier goodbye in January 1958. He flew to New York to star in *The Entertainer* on Broadway opposite Joan Plowright. Although they put on a public front of togetherness, Vivien and Olivier were leading separate lives.

BELOW: In 1959, Vivien made her one and only foray into television acting in a live performance of *The Skin of Our Teeth* on the British network ITV. She is pictured here with George Devine in the play's third act.

well. For a while it looked as if Elizabeth Taylor's producer husband Mike Todd would provide the money, but he died in a plane crash in March 1958 and the film was shelved completely.

It is easy to mourn what could have been. Considering the stature that Olivier's other Shakespeare films have reached in recent years, there is no doubt that a filmed Leigh-Olivier *Macbeth* would have occupied a unique place in cinema history. But it is doubtful such a film would have helped to preserve their personal relationship. Olivier resumed his role in *The Entertainer* in late 1957 and fell in love with Joan Plowright, who replaced Dorothy Tutin as Jean Rice. Plowright, then twenty-eight and fresh out of the Bristol Old Vic Theatre School, was in many ways the antithesis of Vivien. In her Olivier saw an opportunity to embark on a new career and a new life. According to John Osborne, Olivier's revelation sent Vivien into "an almost unbroken condition of shock."

Vivien's aptitude for love and her want for friendship saw her through the next two years following her estrangement from Olivier. Her magnetism, coupled with the courage and humility to face those she harmed during her manic episodes, was what made people stick. "Vivien was really lucky in her friends and relationships," Hester St. John-Ives says. "She had that mesmeric effect that made you want to be on her side." Vivien inspired strong devotion in others, sometimes finding it in the most surprising corners. In April 1958, she opened in *Duel of Angels* at the Apollo Theatre on Shaftesbury Avenue, directed by Jean-Louis Barrault. Playing the good angel opposite her wicked one was Claire Bloom, who had been intimate with Olivier during the filming of *Richard III*. Bloom grew up admiring Vivien; *Gone With the Wind* was her favorite film. In spite of her brief affair with Olivier, Vivien showed her nothing but affection and kindness. She thought Vivien "a better stage actress than she was given credit for," and remembers her today as "a lovely, fragile, beautiful human being."

John Osborne became another unlikely ally. He spent evenings with Vivien while Olivier performed at the Palace Theatre and she would often take him to dinner or to the cinema. "Vivien's virtue, always a prized one in my book, was enthusiasm," he wrote, "the physical expression of hope, the antidote to despair and that most deadly of sins, sloth." Osborne was loyal to Olivier yet sympathetic toward Vivien and was able to view the situation objectively: "However much one sympathized with Olivier's desperation to escape the destruction of her magic alchemy, it was impossible not to be affected . . . by the pain cascading over both of them."

VIVIEN LEIGH and CLAIRE BLOOM in *DUEL OF ANGELS*

LEFT: Vivien continued to entertain at Notley Abbey. Pictured L-R: Olivier's niece Dinah Day, Colin Clark, Leigh Holman, Vivien, Louise Olivier, and Sabina the corgi, summer 1958.

ABOVE: Vivien and Claire Bloom star in *Duel of Angels*, 1958. Bloom greatly admired Vivien.

RIGHT: Vivien as Lulu in Noël Coward's *Look After Lulu!* 1959.

PLAYS AND PLAYERS

VIVIEN LEIGH in *LOOK AFTER LULU!* at the New Theatre

The feeling of being discarded for a younger woman tore at Vivien. When Olivier wrote asking for a divorce in October 1958, she replied with dignified but vehement passion from her bed at Leigh Holman's house, "I have come to the conclusion (a fearfully painful one) that a clean and *absolute* break is the only path to follow. So I intend to divorce you on the grounds of Desertion mental & physical . . . I feel confident I shall make my own life & you have *always* made yours." But it wasn't that simple to "let 25 years go lightly."

Olivier called on Vivien's friends to rally around her. He was going to Hollywood to film *Spartacus*

for Stanley Kubrik and didn't plan on coming back to Vivien. Some, like Lauren Bacall, understood. Bacall came to London in 1958 following Humphrey Bogart's death and formed a close-knit trio with Vivien and comedic actress Kay Kendall. Olivier invited her to lunch at The Ivy and asked her to look after Vivien: "The marriage had been heaven the first ten years—hell the second. Now it was over. But she needed her friends—he wanted me to stand firm and close to her. He felt such concern for her, such pain at the ending of it all. But he knew he would not survive if he did not get away." Others pleaded for Olivier to reconsider. There was Vivien's

LEFT: At the end of their marriage, Olivier asked Vivien's friends to stand firm with her. She is pictured at the Ivy restaurant in Covent Garden with Kay Kendall, Noël Coward, and Lauren Bacall in January 1959.

ABOVE: Vivien spent the 1959 Christmas holiday with Noël Coward at his chalet in Les Avants, Switzerland. Despite often finding her shifting moods difficult to deal with, Coward remained one of Vivien's closest friends. He was also one of the few people who managed to remain neutral about the breakup of Vivien's marriage to Olivier.

health to think about. Could he really move on knowing that Vivien was so unhappy? Olivier divulged his feelings about the situation to his sister-in-law Hester, who, living at Notley, was in the unique position to see both sides of the equation. Olivier had Vivien's best interests in mind, but first and foremost were his own. Something in him had changed and his survival instincts had kicked in. "My heart aches for her," he wrote to Hester, "but I cannot let my mind follow it." Near the end of his life, Olivier looked back on the end of his marriage to Vivien and compared it to a drowning person reaching out to someone else in a life raft. "I said, I'm sorry, I can't pull you out. If I pull you out, you'll pull me in."

For Vivien, things would get worse before they got better. Within the span of four months, she lost two people near to her heart. In September 1959, Kay Kendall died of leukemia at age thirty-two. Her father, Ernest Hartley, passed away in December. That Christmas Vivien sought refuge at Noël Coward's chalet in Les Avants, Switzerland. Since July she had been playing in his *Look After Lulu!*, "because it was expedient." Now she was thankful for his "unfailing friendship" and for making Christmas and the New Year "so much more possible than I ever thought it could be."

Although Coward had often expressed his frustration with her emotional ups and downs, he remained one of Vivien's closest friends. Her courage during this obviously difficult time moved him greatly: "Vivien, with deep sadness in her heart and, for one fleeting moment, tears in her eyes,

behaved gaily and charmingly and never for one instant allowed her private happiness to spill over . . . . I have always been fond of her in spite of her former exigency and frequent tiresomeness, but last night my fondness was fortified by profound admiration and respect for her strength of character."

Then in February 1960, a Canadian couple bought Vivien's beloved Notley Abbey. After Dickie Olivier's death in 1958 the farm became difficult to manage, and with Olivier's continuous absence it made little sense not to put it on the market. She wrote to Tarquin Olivier:

"It has been a most wretched and miserable time . . . I walk from place to precious place and gaze at the beloved views with tears pouring down my face. What memories for all one's life—such unbelievable rare happiness, sweetness and quietude there has been here. I don't forget the other times too, but they seem to me outweighed by blissful togetherness. Dear God it is a heartache . . . Oh the hundreds of times my beloved Larry and I have wandered here in wonder and grateful amazement at the beauty all around us—the feeling that we were a little responsible for creating it too made it all so doubly dear."

The house had been Vivien's haven for the past fifteen years—a place of joy and fantasy, an emblem of love, and a shelter from the outside world during times of personal difficulty. She'd "known for some time that it would have to go," but it didn't make parting any easier. With Notley went her last hope of salvaging her marriage.

Olivier would remain the love of Vivien's life. Pictured in Los Angeles, February 1957.

CHAPTER 8

TWILIGHT

"I know everyone has to face periods of despondency and that one must not always trust everyone, or else one can be very hurt. At the same time, I have learned who really are my friends, and that can be very comforting, and gives one confidence for whatever lies ahead."

—Vivien Leigh to Godfrey Winn, 1964

The Oliviers's divorce marked the end of an era. For twenty years they had resided on the upper echelon of celebrity culture, representing idyllic romance and offering a glamorous antidote to dreary, postwar austerity. That they appeared to be an exception to the typical, short-lived Hollywood marriage only elevated their stature in the eyes of their admirers. Although there had been speculation of a breakup for many years, the demise of show business's most revered couple sent shock waves around the world. Though fraught with turbulence in private, the marriage had seemed, to many on the outside, to be "eternal and unchanging."

Vivien mourned for what she and Olivier once had, rather than what their relationship became in the end. Had he stayed, neither would have been happy, but a significant part of Vivien's very identity had been bound up with him. Now, for the first time in her adult life, she found herself alone. She was painted as a desolate, tragic figure. The press tended toward the melodramatic. A headline printed in *Modern Screen* read, "This is Vivien

This is Your Life: Vivien was delighted when the company threw her a surprise forty-eighth birthday party on November 5, 1961.

Leigh today: 'After living half my life with Larry, he suddenly left me for a younger woman.'" The tabloid *Daily Mirror* made sure to highlight the fact that she wept in divorce court. During the split, many of their mutual friends took sides. Vivien's journalist friend Godfrey Winn remembered those who "sought misguidedly to show their sympathy for the vacuum in which Vivien temporarily found herself," by criticizing Olivier. "They were making a grave error to do so. For nothing displeased or alienated her more."

Vivien required psychiatric assistance to help her cope with the unbearable pain of losing the love of her life. Yet she understood—even if she never accepted—why Olivier left, and this did not diminish her obsessive devotion toward him. In a letter dated June 20, 1960, she wrote to him with sound mind:

"Whatever happens let us be friends my dearest one. Conachy [her London psychiatrist] has done a very marvelous thing for me & I am feeling as I have not felt for many many years. Perhaps all the interim mistakes have made just too much difference for our life together, I do not know . . . I feel very deeply in love with Jack [Merivale] & very dearly grateful to him but it does not alter the fact that I shall love you all my life & with a tenderness and respect that is all embracing. I understand very well how difficult—even impossible it had become—though lack of knowledge as to how to heal it let us face that. Well now that is accomplished & I hope my life will prove a useful & good one, to many people."

Although Olivier moved on, marrying Joan Plowright in 1961 and starting a new family, the ties between Vivien and him were never severed completely. And this is perhaps why Vivien never "really believed that he wouldn't come back" to her. They still shared many of the same friends and colleagues. Peter Hiley, the jack-of-all-trades who later took on a diplomatic role with the estates of both families, often saw both of them on the same day. He told Olivier's biographer Terry Coleman, "At Eaton Square [Vivien] would say, 'have you heard from him this morning? Is he all right? Did he sleep well?' Then I went round to Larry, and he would ask, 'Puss all right? Did she have enough breakfast?'" They remained monetarily connected, as well. As part of the divorce settlement, Vivien collected £3,350 tax-free per year on Olivier's life-insurance policy. It enabled her to live comfortably in her flat at 54 Eaton Square in London's fashionable Belgravia district for the remainder of her days. They continued to exchange phone calls, birthday wishes, and letters. Sometimes, when Vivien was going through a particularly difficult period, Olivier would pay her a visit. Hester St. John-Ives and her daughter Louise were staying with Vivien on one particular occasion when Olivier drove up from Brighton to have lunch at her country home, Tickerage Mill. "He gave her every reason to think that he wanted to be there," Hester says. Louise still remembers the meal that was served and how, in her excitement and nervousness, Vivien wanted to make sure that everything was in perfect order:

"It was a can of pears, roast beef, fresh raspberries. And I do remember she was very nervous. When he arrived she wouldn't come downstairs to start off with, but she did. She came down, and then, actually, it went really well. I remember walking around the garden with them. They talked a lot about roses and the garden because she was a very keen gardener . . . and they talked about the old days, mutual friends, and Notley. I think it was a happy visit. I don't think she thought it was going to be reconciliation or anything like that, but it just really mattered a lot to her that he was coming."

LEFT: Vivien photographed in London shortly before her divorce from Olivier, 1960.

RIGHT: To many, the Olivier's marriage had seemed "constant and unchanging." Their divorce in December 1960 shocked many of their fans and friends alike.

FILMJOURNALEN

Oscarvinnaren LAURENCE OLIVIER med fru och katt. (Den förra: Vivien Leigh.) Se vårt stora reportage på sid. 10—12.

Färgfoto: Keystone

"I shall never marry again, I am certain of that," Vivien told Godfrey Winn. "Larry still possesses too much of me. But as long as I'm well enough to go on working, I shall be alright." Indeed, it was in work that she found solace and her silver lining. In April 1960, *Duel of Angels* was transferred to Broadway under Robert Helpmann's direction. John Osborne's wife Mary Ure took over for Claire Bloom. In the role of Armand was John "Jack" Merivale, who would become, in many ways, Vivien's lifesaver. A 6'5" lanky brunette with sharp features and an Oxford education, Merivale was four years Vivien's junior and came from a theatrical family. His parents were both actors, as was his stepmother, Gladys Cooper, and at one time his stepbrother, John Buckmaster—Vivien's troubled former lover. "Any ass who can't do anything else becomes an actor," Vivien declared on David Susskind's television show *Open End* in May 1960. Acting was something Jack Merivale naturally fell into but he never had ambitions of greatness—it was his life but it was not what he lived for. He occasionally made forays into cinema in the 1950s and '60s, playing supporting parts in films like Roy Ward Baker's *A Night to Remember* and *Arabesque* with Gregory Peck and Sophia Loren.

Merivale had known Vivien casually since 1937, when he was an understudy for *A Midsummer Night's Dream* at the Old Vic. In 1940, he played Balthasar in the ill-fated *Romeo and Juliet* and spent a weekend with Vivien and Olivier at Snedens Landing in New York. There he caught a glimpse of Vivien's mercurial personality when she suddenly accused him of cheating at a game of Chinese checkers and attempting to come between her and Olivier. "We've been together four years now and nobody's going to come between us," she'd cried. From what Merivale knew at the time, he believed their relationship to be inseparable. That was why, in 1960, he paid no

LEFT: Vivien mourned the happiness that she and Olivier had once had. Pictured at Durham Cottage with their Siamese cat New Boy in 1946.

RIGHT: Leigh Holman remained a constant friend throughout Vivien's life, and offered support when her marriage ended. She is pictured here with Holman and Olivier's niece, Louise, at Zeals, Holman's house in Wilshire, circa 1961.

Vivien found solace and companionship in her final years with actor Jack Merivale. They are pictured here together after a performance of *Duel of Angels*, 1960.

Vivien photographed in her dressing room while making up for a performance of *Duel of Angels*. A picture of Olivier can be seen on her dressing table. Los Angeles, 1960.

mind to rumors of divorce. Even when Vivien made it clear during rehearsals for *Duel of Angels* that she was interested in him, he felt uneasy about pursuing anything beyond friendship: "It really wasn't until she came off the play and after those treatments with Conachy that there was no doubt in my mind," Merivale told Anne Edwards. "Before that there was great doubt—of course there was. But apart from that, she was a married woman."

It was Merivale who helped Vivien come to terms with the end of her marriage. On May 21, 1960, Vivien dropped a "birthday bombshell"

when she publicly announced that Olivier had "asked for a divorce, in order to marry Miss Joan Plowright." She would "naturally do whatever he wishes." Olivier read the statement in the newspaper the next morning—his fifty-third birthday—and "felt that it was intended as a black-hearted birthday present." There was fear that his and Plowright's relationship would now be seen as collusion under the law, thereby preventing a divorce from happening. Olivier wrote to Vivien and received an apologetic letter from Merivale in return. Vivien had been in a manic state and was coerced by journalist David Lewin (with whom she had spoken several times before) into making an official announcement. Merivale tried to dissuade Lewin from being alone with Vivien as he "didn't feel this was any time for her to be talking with the press." Vivien ignored him. Later, when she was well again, Vivien asked Merivale to write and explain the situation to Olivier. "She was in agonies of doubt about it and confessed that she couldn't remember doing it or how it came about." Merivale wanted Olivier to know the truth and didn't want him to "think that it was done vindictively or with calculation." He then told Olivier that he no longer had doubts about his feelings for Vivien and he was certain that they could make a happy life together.

In personality, Merivale could not have been more different from his predecessor. He has been described as a kind, gentle, and passive character. "She was very tough with him because she was still

in love with Olivier until the end of her life," John Gielgud recalled. Merivale loved Vivien deeply but displayed no jealousy at the thought of coming in second to the memory of Olivier. It was a situation he accepted because he wouldn't have shared the same level of intimacy with Vivien otherwise. They had many arguments, but Merivale was never anxious around her. During her bad times, he was not afraid to step in, making her see the doctor when she didn't want to, sometimes forcing her to have ECT against her will, and keeping her off the stage when she posed a danger to herself and others, as in the case of the 1963 musical *Tovarich*. Merivale stood resolute, providing emotional stability when Vivien needed it most, and she, in turn, gave him

---

Vivien became a grandmother in December 1958. She is pictured here with her mother Gertrude Hartley (left), daughter Suzanne Farrington, and baby Neville.

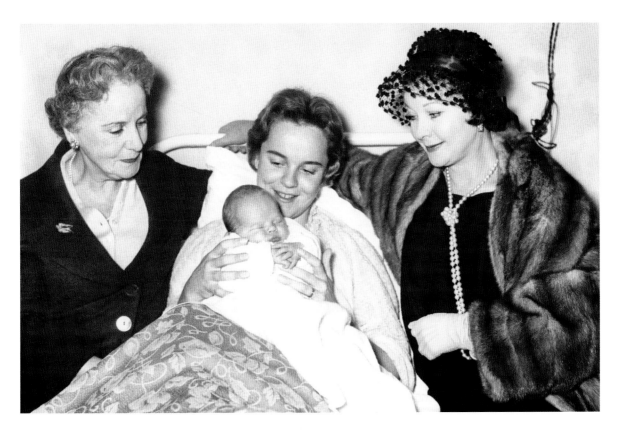

First-time director José Quintero goes over a crucial scene
with Vivien on the set of *The Roman Spring of Mrs. Stone.*

some of his most cherished moments. "No one
could ever know how happy it was on the rare
occasions that we were alone together," he said.
With Merivale as her anchor, Vivien slowly picked
up the pieces of her life and moved forward. Parting from Olivier allowed her to rediscover her own
identity and to set out on her own path, away from
his immense shadow.

It is difficult not to draw parallels between
Vivien Leigh the woman and the characters she
played on screen during the 1960s, and for the first
time audiences would have recognized this without
the benefit of hindsight. The 1961 film *The Roman
Spring of Mrs. Stone*, based on the novella of the
same title by Tennessee Williams, is a story about
the fears of aging and loneliness. Screenwriter
Gavin Lambert remembers how he, Williams, and
first-time director José Quintero considered a list
of possible actresses for the title character, Karen
Stone, but none seemed suitable. "Then, one day
Tennessee said, 'Vivien must play it.' We immediately realized she was ideal." When first

Karen Stone is wooed by gigolo Paolo di Leo (Beatty) in
The Roman Spring of Mrs. Stone.

LEFT: A publicity portrait of Vivien and Warren Beatty in *The Roman Spring of Mrs. Stone* (1961).

Vivien received good reviews for her performance as Tennessee Williams's aging actress Karen Stone. Many American critics hoped it would be the beginning of a new career for Vivien on the Hollywood screen.

In 1961, Vivien traveled to Atlanta for the Civil War centennial and *Gone With the Wind* re-premiere. Twenty-two years had passed and she and Olivia de Havilland were the only surviving main cast members. It was a moving experience.

ABOVE: Vivien loved wearing wigs, and used one to put the younger cast members of the Old Vic world tour at ease on their first meeting. She is pictured here circa 1961.

RIGHT: Vivien as Marguerite Gauthier in Alexandre Dumas, fil's *The Lady of the Camellias*. Australia, 1961.

approached, Vivien declined the role. She was familiar with the book and "found the portrait of an aging actress exploited by an Italian gigolo too 'cruel' and too 'grotesque,'" Lambert said. "Then she read the script and changed her mind."

Karen Stone is an actress approaching fifty who was once the talk of the town and who suddenly finds herself too old for the ingénue roles that made her famous. She flees public scrutiny and settles in Rome after the death of her husband. Karen is set up and eventually falls in love with young and beautiful Paolo di Leo (Warren Beatty), a gigolo known for preying on wealthy, older American women. The prospect of being alone and "drifting" through middle age is so frightening to Karen that she endures Paolo's unkind remarks

and attempts at extortion. She attempts to recapture her youth in order to keep his attention, degrading herself in the process.

It was appreciated that Vivien, unlike Karen Stone, was not afraid to act her own age on screen. *TIME* magazine felt she brought "grace and dignity to a role that, as written, comes depressingly close to a portrait of a lecher as a middle-aged woman." Critics who had followed Vivien's career and the public saga of her recent divorce noted that she used her own experience to bring realistic vulnerability to her character. "No one can sit on a banquet in a swank restaurant and watch a churlish lover walk away with another woman more knowingly and poignantly than she," Bosley Crowther wrote. "Her surges of ardor have the fullness and fitfulness of the real thing; her torrents of grief are as liquid as though they came from a heart truly crushed." *Hollywood Citizen News* hoped it would be "the beginning of [Vivien's] 'new' career on the American screen."

Although she was still considered one of the greatest actresses and beauties working in the business, Vivien did share Karen Stone's fear of becoming undesirable. She always fought to be recognized for her talent, but she more than anyone was aware of the significant role her looks had played in her success. According to Warren Beatty

TOP LEFT: Vivien as Marguerite and Jack Merivale as Armand Duval in *The Lady of the Camellias*. Australia, 1961.

LEFT: Vivien as Viola, disguised as Cesario, in Shakespeare's *Twelfth Night*. Australia, 1961.

RIGHT: Vivien as *Twelfth Night*'s Viola, in all her splendor. Photographed by Angus McBean for the 1961 Old Vic world tour.

TOP LEFT: Cast member Carolyn Pertwee snapped this photograph of Vivien and Jack Merivale on the plane from Melbourne to Brisbane, 1961.

BOTOM LEFT: Vivien manages the barbeque during a beach picnic for the company at Surfer's Paradise. Brisbane, 1961.

BELOW: Vivien was invited to stay with several notable people in Australia in 1961. She is pictured here leaving the island of Rottnest off the coast of Freemantle, where she and Jack Merivale had been visiting with a count.

biographer Suzanne Finstad, everyone on the set was convinced that Vivien was attracted to her younger costar—who had recently made his screen debut in *Splendor in the Grass* with Natalie Wood—and was jealous of his girlfriend at the time, Joan Collins. She also felt insecure around Jill St. John, who played Barbara Bingham, the airy starlet for whom Paolo leaves Karen. "I was a great fan," St. John said of Vivien, not unkindly. "I mean, who hadn't seen *Gone With the Wind*? And she was very beautiful . . . she didn't speak to me for the entire film. She just nodded. That was it, for all those weeks. But I got to watch a great actress."

In March 1961, José Quintero granted Vivien time off from filming to travel to Atlanta for the Civil War centennial and *Gone With the Wind* re-premiere. More than twenty years had passed

since the film's initial release, and many who had attended the original premiere in 1939 now brought their children and grandchildren to see Scarlett O'Hara—now a grandmother herself—in person. It was a bittersweet homecoming. She, Olivia de Havilland, and David O. Selznick were the only surviving key figures from the film. Olivia de Havilland remembers, "One could not help but think of Leslie Howard, who was not with us in 1939 but in England, the European phase of WWII having already broken out in September of that year—a war which, in 1943, eventually claimed his life under heroic and tragic circumstances. I also could not help thinking of Clark Gable, who had died shortly before . . . Margaret Mitchell, too, was gone, having lost her life in 1949 in a tragic way."

Vivien was shocked when, on her arrival from London, Reuters correspondent Joe Greenidge (who admitted to never having seen *Gone With the Wind*) asked her which character she'd played in the film. "The picture has been released for 22 years and the book even longer. If you don't know what part I played, the interview is over," she told him. Though the exchange was brushed off with a laugh, the story made headlines. She was considered brave for returning to the scene of her first major film success, now that she was forty-seven and no longer in her youthful glory. "Twenty-one years! There are girls calling themselves actresses who weren't even born when Vivien, already 26, was in the springtime of her career," the *Daily Express* reported. To this Vivien gave a poised response. The key to longevity lay in dedication and hard work. "Being a film star—just a film star—is such a false life living for false values," she said.

LEFT: While in Australia in 1961, Vivien was painted by artist Paul Fitzgerald.

BOTTOM LEFT: Vivien and Louise Kirtland in *Tovarich*, 1963.

BOTTOM RIGHT: Director Delbert Mann, Vivien, and Jean-Pierre Aumont do a script read-through of the musical comedy *Tovarich* in Philadelphia, 1963.

"Actresses go on for a long time and there are always marvelous parts to play. Film stars have short professional lives usually. But I don't ever want to retire—I want to act until I'm 90."

Over the next three years, Vivien became a citizen of the world. In the summer of 1961, she set off with the Old Vic on a tour that included Australia, New Zealand, and several countries in Central and South America. Her friend Robert Helpmann was assigned to direct, and as the company leader, Vivien was given carte blanche over which plays they performed. She chose *Twelfth Night* and *Duel of Angels*, two recent personal favorites. The third addition was Alexandre Dumas, fil's *The Lady of the Camellias*, fulfilling her own long-held wish of playing the tragic, consumptive Marguerite Gautier.

The company rehearsed for two months at the Finsbury Park Empire before embarking on their journey. Many of the cast members were younger and nervous about meeting Vivien for the first time. Carolyn Pertwee, who played Gilly in *Duel of Angels* and understudied the role of Viola in *Twelfth Night*, thought that Vivien had a unique way of putting everyone at ease: "I remember sitting on the floor around her because there weren't that many seats. We were talking about hair, and she suddenly whisked off a wig from her head and said, 'I always wear this. It's so easy in the morning. I just get up and put it on.' It was fabulous and looked very cute. That was very disarming."

Vivien's return to Australia created a surge of public interest, although journalists who had covered the tour with Olivier in 1948 were now spiteful toward Jack Merivale. "It was horrible, really," Pertwee recalls. They would say things like, "Who is

ABOVE: Vivien rehearses for one of her song and dance numbers, 1963.

RIGHT: Vivien and Byron Mitchell dance the Charleston in *Tovarich*. Broadway, 1963.

Noël Coward congratulates Vivien after a performance of *Tovarich* on Broadway, 1963.

he and what's he done?" Merivale took the criticism in stride. Vivien was the undisputed star of the tour. All of the actors and technical crew were "aware of her, of who she was, and one was a little bit in awe of her. She was not intentionally intimidating. You just were respectful. And we didn't call her Vivien, we called her 'Miss Leigh.'"

When the company arrived in Melbourne for the start of the tour, there were no scheduled rest days. A rehearsal was called at 10:00 the next morning and the only person who turned up was Vivien. Everyone else had overslept due to jetlag. Vivien acquired her professional discipline in the

theater from Olivier. "He taught me more about how actors should be, about how an actor should live, than anybody I can imagine," she said in 1960. The tour's Chief Technician, Coeks Gordon, remembers, "When we would arrive in each theater she would ask me to gather the crews together, and then I would introduce her to everyone. She also asked me to find out any particular facts regarding the crew members and she would

then ask them about it." Afterward, Gordon went on to work as production manager of the National Theatre Company at the Old Vic and observed Olivier employing the same personal method of acknowledgement.

Vivien's warm generosity was endearing. She refused invitations to big gatherings unless both cast and crew were allowed to attend, and she enjoyed handing out personalized gifts: monogramed ties for the men and Balenciaga scarves for the women. She was also "a great one for writing letters. So, if you got a gift, you must write her a thank you letter. She would expect that," Carolyn Pertwee says. "In fact, we were all told we should write to thank her, which of course we then did. We then got another letter back thanking us for the letter thanking her." Her bigheartedness was repaid in Sydney when the entire company gathered to throw her a surprise forty-eighth birthday party resembling the TV program *This Is Your Life*, complete with costumes, cabaret, and a souvenir book. According to actor David Dodimead, "forty years fell off her face when she realized" what was happening.

The tour received good notices, in general, and it was thought that Vivien had "gained in reassurance, technique and versatility" since 1948. *Lady of the Camellias* was soundly praised and *Theater World* hoped Vivien would play Marguerite Gautier in London, where she was sure to "be greeted with applause likely to recall memories of that historic occasion at the Ambassadors in 1935 when in a single evening she leapt from obscurity to stardom." As she had with Olivier thirteen years earlier, Vivien was expected to act the part of ambassador and attend a barrage of tiring official functions. By the time the company reached Mexico in early 1962, she was showing signs of impending mania.

Actors Mark Kingston and Marigold Sharman thought that Vivien "could be simply enchanting and then cause great distress in the company because of silly actions." There was one particular incident that they both remembered for years afterward. The company was invited to a party thrown by a wealthy man in Rio de Janeiro, the last stop on the tour. As the guests walked up the drive to the hacienda, a line of school children showered them with flower petals. Many distinguished Brazilians were apparently in attendance and Vivien thought the whole thing a bore. Marigold Sharman was enjoying the party when Jack Merivale suddenly took hold of her arm and said, "'Marigold, you have to come, she's getting funny.' And [Vivien] had laid herself out on the floor. She was laid out as though in the fainting position and then the one eye opened and she said, 'Marigold, I have to get out!'" Vivien apologized to her distraught host, saying she was too overwhelmed by the excitement of it all and that she had to leave.

When they got into the car she instructed Merivale to drive to a restaurant so they could enjoy themselves. "The man must have discovered this happened because he would have known everything that was going on," Mark Kingston recalled. "Oh it was just grizzly but I suppose that was what made her what she was. She was so quixotic and changeable . . ." Said Merivale, "We got out of Rio by the skin of our teeth."

While performing in Auckland, Vivien had received a surprise phone call from American producer Abel Farbman. He invited her to play Tatiana, an exiled Russian Grand Duchess working as a maid in Paris, in a musical version of the Jacques Deval and Robert E. Sherwood comedy *Tovarich*. Vivien had seen and enjoyed the 1937 film starring Claudette Colbert and Charles Boyer, but she hesitated to accept the part. She was an actress, not a singer. What made Farbman think she could pull off a Broadway musical? "This is the age of the non-singing singer," the producer said. "I need an actress who can convincingly impersonate a Grand Duchess. To be sure, she must sing five or six songs, but the lyric demands of the role are secondary to its acting requirements. Remember, this isn't *Aida*." Farbman was so intent on having Vivien in his production that he flew to New Zealand to meet her personally. Charmed by the song recordings Farbman gave her, Vivien decided to give it a try. It was a huge gamble, she knew, but the challenge might reap rewards. In Wellington, she gave a small audition on stage at the Opera House, singing Irving Berlin's "Always," with the accompaniment of a lone pianist. After following her to Buenos Aires, Farbman returned to New York with Vivien's signature on the contract.

"If anybody had told me a year ago that I would be returning to the Broadway stage in a musical comedy, I would have said that person was out of his mind. But here I am!" Rehearsals for *Tovarich* began in Philadelphia in December 1962. Vivien had already undergone weeks of rigorous preparation. There were daily singing lessons and choreography practice, as well as script run-throughs with her leading man, Jean-Pierre Aumont. She was quoted as saying that it "felt good to be doing something new," but in reality the demands of appearing in this new medium

Vivien received a Tony Award for her performance as Grand Duchess Tatiana in *Tovarich*. Pictured with the other winners (L–R): Zero Mostel from *A Funny Thing Happened on the Way to the Forum*, Vivien, Uta Hagen, and Arthur Hill from *Who's Afraid of Virginia Woolf?*

threw her into depression. "You must not think that I despair all the time," Vivien wrote to Merivale on December 28. He was busy filming *The List of Adrian Messenger* for John Huston and had been unable to accompany Vivien to America. "These rehearsals are so unlike anything one has known that it is difficult to get an overall picture. They keep saying that Philadelphia and Boston do not matter but they *do* to me." By the beginning of the run, Vivien was having "an utterly wretched time" and asked Peter Glenville to take over from Delbert Mann as director. She had little faith in the way the play was shaping up and was worried they wouldn't have enough time to get it right before New York. "Admittedly we did a marvelous week's business & the audiences do seem to enjoy it but anyone whose opinion one values says it just will not do for Broadway, and this, as you know, I have felt all along."

The addition of new scenes for the Broadway premiere didn't help matters. Vivien found it difficult to eat and sleep, and was plagued by mental and physical exhaustion. "I am assailed by fears of what would happen if it should turn out to be a failure," she wrote on February 6. "I should never have taken on something so foreign. It is another world all together." Dr. Conachy intervened by sending her medication but in March, when they finally reached New York, Vivien had yet to rise out of her dispirited mood. She had successfully passed through Philadelphia and Boston without incurring the wrath of critics, and advance ticket sales at the Broadway Theatre looked promising. Merivale urged her to adopt some of her colleagues' confidence in the show's success.

"I must confess to you that I have never felt so

mortally ill & I wonder each performance how I shall manage. . . . I think the critics will be brutal (I shall agree with them) but the thing may run." *Tovarich* opened at the Broadway Theatre on March 18. The production itself was panned for being "routine" and failing to transmit the "wit and gaiety" of the Deval and Sherwood play. Jean-Pierre Aumont, whom Vivien had known for many years but had difficulty working with, was "not much of a singer and runs entirely out of vocal steam before the evening is out."

Despite her conviction in the failure of both the play and her own performance, Vivien captivated critics. "How lucky [*Tovarich*] is to have Miss Leigh to give it regality and lightness," remarked Howard Taubman of *The New York Times*, who thought she made the transition to musical comedy with "the greatest of ease." The New York correspondent for the London *Times* thought that Vivien had a gift "for expressing a character" and that "a sort of explosion takes place when this expression finds a new form . . . The explosion is all the greater when Miss Leigh lights the fuse with her highly personal charm in an impersonally overproduced production." For her efforts, Vivien was awarded Broadway's highest honor, a Tony Award for Best Performance by a Leading Actress in a Musical. She continued to keep *Tovarich* afloat until October 1963, when a recurrence of mania forced her to bow out and return to London for treatment.

Vivien spent some time recovering in a nursing home in St. John's Wood and at her flat in Eaton Square before retreating to Tickerage Mill, the picturesque Queen Anne-style house she had purchased three years earlier at the suggestion of actor Dirk Bogarde. It was here, tucked away in a valley near the village of Blackboys in Sussex that Vivien found solace and quietude after the upheaval of her divorce from Olivier. The millpond in back of the house provided the essential, soothing element of water and the walled garden was filled with her favorite white flowers. Vivien's green thumb is still apparent today. Tickerage's current owners have named it "Vivien's White Garden."

Vivien's residency at Tickerage sent a wave of excitement rippling through the area. One day, not long after moving in, she opened the door to find two shy neighborhood children with autograph books and box brownie cameras waiting outside. They were ten-year-old Rod Hall, who would grow up to become a well-known literary agent, and his sister Ann. The Hall children were too young to have seen any of Vivien's films, but she signed their books and invited them to return the next day to snap a photograph of her in the garden. Rod Hall later wrote that he was "thrilled and flattered that this beautiful, grownup woman had actually given me—a little kid from the village—an appointment as if I were also grownup, also important. That was how she made me feel, how Vivien would always make me feel. Important, special, interesting."

From then on Vivien took Rod and Ann under her wing, inviting them to ride in her Rolls-Royce whenever a famous acquaintance needed picking up at Uckfield train station. She entertained often, and her own grandchildren visited occasionally, but Rod said he and his sister never felt excluded. She gave Rod special access to a good fishing spot and kept her pond stocked with trout. Ann was allowed to experiment with her makeup and perfume. She showed them her *Gone With the Wind* Oscar, which she kept in her bathroom. "Just something I

Vivien pictured on the day she moved in to Tickerage Mill, the beautiful Queen Anne house in Sussex, April 27, 1961.

won," she said, offhandedly. Vivien was so "kind and friendly" to them that they often "forgot she was so famous, and just thought of her as our neighbor."

In the summer of 1964, thirty years after her first screen appearance, Vivien returned to Hollywood to make what would be her last film. Producer-director Stanley Kramer had Vivien specifically in mind when he adapted Katherine Anne Porter's novel *Ship of Fools* for the screen, and proof of her lasting star power was evident in the fact that she received top billing among an ensemble cast that included two of the era's biggest names, Lee Marvin and Simone Signoret. Vivien admired Kramer's work and he was the sole reason she agreed to take the job. Porter's magnum opus about a colorful group of passengers traveling from Mexico to Germany in 1933 had proved unreadable, in Vivien's opinion.

"What's happening, is that roles come few and far between when an actress gets older," Vivien was quoted as saying. "In the past, and particularly in London, producers, playwrights, and directors would think nothing of casting a woman in her forties or fifties to portray a heroine in her twenties. These days, age has become such a factor. . . . The times have changed, I suppose." Although Vivien's observation was certainly accurate, Kramer believed that her inability to find good roles at this point in her life had more to do with unreliability

---

George Cukor remained a lifelong friend of Vivien's. When she went to Hollywood in 1964, Cukor, Katharine Hepburn, and Simone Signoret helped to look after her. Cukor is pictured visiting Vivien on the set of her last film, *Ship of Fools*, at Columbia studios.

than age. She posed too much of a financial risk because producers never knew if she'd be able to deliver a full performance. But Kramer didn't regret casting her in his film. He admired her fortitude, later saying, "She had health problems. She was taking shock treatments. She was highly nervous, but despite her illness, didn't let it intrude. She would occasionally go off to one side and actually be shaking, master control over herself, go back to the scene, manage it and do it, and then go back to the palpitation again. It was something which is indescribable."

While filming, Vivien lived with Merivale in a rented house in the Hollywood Hills, high above Los Angeles. John Gielgud became a third housemate while making *The Loved One* and closely observed Vivien's moods. He thought that playing a supporting role for the first time irritated her because she felt like she was "slipping and getting old." Gielgud even informed Olivier about his experience staying with Vivien. Katharine Hepburn, George Cukor, and Simone Signoret were around often and seemed to take good care of her, he said, though he knew Olivier was aware how "terribly difficult" it was for Merivale to keep up with her manic energy. Simone Signoret remembered Vivien as a nostalgic figure: "She was no longer Laurence Olivier's wife, but she wanted to remain Lady Olivier. She asked us to dress and my little wandering sables worked hard at her house. The dinners were served by the light of candelabra. . . . At the end of these evenings the phonograph played the theme from *Gone With the Wind*. It made her sad, but she did it deliberately . . ."

In 1981, writing of the luminescent actors of Hollywood's golden age, film historian John Kobal described Vivien as an "extraordinary star, unsentimental, detached, neither asking nor giving nor expecting sympathy for herself or her characters." Never was this truer than in *Ship of Fools*. Mary Treadwell is a forty-six-year-old divorcee from Virginia whose husband has left her. Embittered and lonely, she drinks and flirts her way through the voyage in a desperate attempt to recapture her youth and desirability. Stanley Kramer was sure Vivien "realized that, in the picture, she was playing something like her own life, and yet she never, by word or gesture, betrayed any such recognition." She didn't need to. Using the camera as her confidant, Vivien bared her vulnerability to the world.

In the film's most powerful scene, Mary Treadwell sits in front of the vanity mirror in her cabin, her reflection the only witness to the performance about to transpire. "You are not young, Mrs. Treadwell," she mutters, applying a thick layer of lipstick. "You have not been young for years. You just didn't want to grow up. Behind those old eyes, you hide a sixteen-year-old heart. Poor fool." Suddenly the camera stands in place of the mirror, revealing Mary's true age, and the physical measures Vivien took in creating this character: false eyelashes, poorly penciled-in eyebrows, and lips drawn on too large. Vivien's performance in this scene evokes glimpses of Scarlett O'Hara, Blanche DuBois, and Karen Stone, until finally she, herself is revealed. As Mary regards her heavily painted appearance in the mirror, she has an epiphany. Recalling an earlier exchange with the younger ship's officer she has strung along throughout the voyage, Mary realizes that if she doesn't "grow up," accept her age, and stop living in the past, she will end up "sitting in a café with a paid escort."

What could easily have been a pitiful moment is instead turned into one of catharsis and empowerment when Denny (Lee Marvin) drunkenly bursts into Mary's room and attempts to have his way with her. Unlike Blanche DuBois or Karen Stone, Mary doesn't succumb to Denny's callous brutality. When she learns that he has been sent to her cabin as a cruel joke, she chases him out into the hallway, beating him across the face with the heel of her stiletto. At the end of the film, she and Denny separately disembark the ship, his face covered in Band-Aids while she coolly walks down the gangway, her head held high. Thus Mary, and subsequently Vivien are able to make a grand exit—from the ship and from filmdom—having left an indelible mark.

One of Vivien's last Hollywood publicity portraits, taken in 1964.

LEGACY

"Give us courage and gaiety and the quiet mind . . . strength to encounter that which is to come, that we may be brave in peril, constant in tribulation, temperate in wrath, and in all changes of fortune, and, down to the gates of death loyal and loving, one to the other."

—One of Vivien's favorite quotes, from *We Thank Thee* by Robert Louis Stevenson

"I am happy now," Vivien told reporter Robert Ottaway in 1965. "I don't think life can be considered in terms of depression and elation. I just don't understand people who say they plan their careers . . . Planning means that the chance opportunity, the unexpected challenge, cannot be seized. And these are the things that make life exciting."

In November of the previous year, Vivien joined publisher Hamish Hamilton and his wife Yvonne on a trip to Frankfurt, Vienna, Istanbul, and Kathmandu before returning to India for the first time since she was six years old. Bombay was the only place she visited that had any connection with her childhood, but "the country, the outlook, the people" fascinated her. Jack Merivale received letters detailing the "unforgettable" beauty of the Himalayas; funeral pyres on the Ganges; friezes of erotica; elephant rides; Buddhist ceremonies and chartering the Raj's plane for a close-up view of Everest. Upon her return Vivien expressed her wish to make a film there—"An Indian film." It was a far-fetched idea but perhaps not entirely. She was a favorite actress of the Indian filmmaker Satyajit Ray.

Life was not without setbacks, but even some of these were the result of seizing challenges. In

Photo by Angus McBean, 1965.

April 1965, Vivien took on the role of a seventy-seven-year-old woman in Paul Osborn's *La Contessa*, based on the novel *The Film of Memory* by Maurice Druon. She wore a bright orange wig and black tape under her eyes as the nostalgic Italian Contessa Sanziani, which didn't appeal to audiences. Alan Dent called it "a sad piece of might-have-been." It was the only play Vivien did in England that never made it onto the London stage.

Ship of Fools premiered in Hollywood in July, earning eight Oscar nominations. Vivien was gracious about not being a nominee herself: "Oh, I've done all that," she said, referring to her Academy Awards for *Gone With the Wind* and *A Streetcar Named Desire*. Instead, she was recognized by the European film community, traveling to Paris where she joined the esteemed company of Anouk Aimee, Brigitte Bardot, Milos Forman, and Alain Resnais to accept the Étoile de Cristal for her performance as Mary Treadwell.

In early 1966, Vivien went to New York to fulfill a long-held dream of appearing in a play by Anton Chekhov. John Gielgud directed and starred with her in *Ivanov*. Despite her character succumbing to tuberculosis at the end of the third act, Gielgud knew that it was Vivien, rather than himself, that audiences and critics came to see. It is ironic that Anna Petrovna should be the last character Vivien played. In May 1967, she came down with what she thought was the flu, only to discover that her old trouble had returned and she had a patch on her lung the size of a human fist.

If Vivien had any inclination of the end drawing near, she didn't let it show. Her death on the night of July 7, 1967 was shocking in its abruptness. The last two months of her life were spent on manda-

tory bed rest while friends and loved ones poured in to 54 Eaton Square, noting that her bedroom resembled the Chelsea Flower Show—a rose bower fit for a queen. She had battled chronic bouts of pulmonary tuberculosis several times over the years, always bouncing back with characteristic optimism. She refused hospital treatment, but she was only fifty-three and no one had reason to believe she wouldn't recover this time.

On her bedside table sat a framed photograph of Olivier and the script for Edward Albee's *A Delicate Balance*. She was set to star opposite her long-time friend Michael Redgrave as Agnes, a middle-aged socialite who feels herself on the brink of madness. Had the play come to fruition, her close friends might again have pointed out the similarities between actress and character. And Vivien may have acknowledged the truth in these words in some way before plunging ahead. After all, life's experience, she said in 1960, was the best tool an actor could have.

The press lamented the loss of "the greatest beauty of her time"; her colleagues in film and theater mourned an actress with grit and determination; moviegoers around the world mourned a luminous star, the eternal Scarlett O'Hara. And those who knew her well—and many who didn't—grieved for a woman who, despite the shadows that often threatened to overwhelm her, enriched their lives in a profound way by simply being present.

In the aftermath of her passing, past discrepancies were forgotten, giving way to tender memo-

---

Vivien studies her script for Paul Osborn's La Contessa, *March 1965.*

ries of a thoughtful, generous friend who admirably refused to be defeated by life's hardships. Katharine Hepburn remembered Vivien as an "exquisite actress, thoughtful, fearless, gracious, and enormously kind . . . a lovely little pink cloud floating through the lives of all her friends, hovering over the setting sun, and thinking of everyone but herself." Noël Coward was poetic, writing to Olivier, "She always reminded me of a bird of paradise. Perhaps now she can find her own."

Olivier had never been far from Vivien's mind. She didn't get a chance to meet his children or to make peace with his new life, though it was not for lack of trying. Vivien wrote several times to Joan Plowright, inviting her and Olivier to Tickerage in February 1965. Vivien's doctors discouraged such meetings. Under normal circumstances it would

have been the mature, harmonious thing to do, but her recurring illness made for very different conditions. In December 1966, Olivier received a letter from psychiatrist S. M. Whitteridge urging him to "sidestep any contact" as that would be the kindest thing for Vivien and the most helpful "from a medical point of view." Olivier was diagnosed with prostate cancer in the spring of 1967 and Vivien was grateful to Joan Plowright for asking Binkie Beaumont to gently break the news to her so that she wouldn't read it in the papers. Thereafter she worried more about Olivier's recovery than she did her own. On the morning of July 8, having received news of Vivien's death, Olivier discharged himself from St. Thomas' Hospital and went to her flat. Jack Merivale left him alone in the bedroom with Vivien. Olivier later revealed that he

LEFT: Vivien accepted the Étoile de Cristal for her performance as Mary Treadwell in *Ship of Fools*. Pictured (L-R): Maurice Ronet, Oskar Werner, Vivien, Georges Auric, Alain Resnais, Brigitte Bardot, Yves Montad, Anouk Aimée, Milos Forman. Paris, November 1966.

ABOVE: Vivien and John Gielgud bundle up against the cold in Connecticut during the pre-New York run of *Ivanov*, 1966.

TOP RIGHT: Vivien visits with director of the Vivien Leigh Society, Don L. McCulty, at the Shubert Theatre in New York after a midnight party at Sardi's. May 8, 1966.

RIGHT: Vivien as Anna Petrovna, her last stage role, in Chekhov's *Ivanov*. She is pictured with John Gielgud, 1966.

had "stood and prayed for forgiveness" for the difficulties that had come between them.

According to her wishes, Vivien was cremated and her ashes scattered on the pond at Tickerage Mill. Her mother Gertrude had a memorial bench erected in the garden at Eaton Square. Borrowing from Shakespeare's *Antony and Cleopatra*, the epitaph reads, "Now boast thee, death, in thy possession lies. A lass unparallel'd."

On August 15, 1967 the luminaries of British stage and screen gathered with Vivien's family at St. Martin-in-the-Fields church in Trafalgar Square to pay their respects. Jack Merivale received letters of sympathy from people in all corners of the entertainment industry, among them actors Van Johnson, Rachel Kempson, Lynn Fontanne, John Mills, David Niven, Ursula Jeans, Robert Helpmann, Celia Johnson, Lilli Palmer, Joyce Carey, and Lauren Bacall; costume designer Lucinda Ballard-Dietz; courtier Victor Stiebel; and wig maker Stanley Hall.

There were other tributes, as well. At 10 p.m. on July 8, theatrical managers in the West End turned off all outside lights for one hour as a sign of respect. Magazine editor Fleur Cowles and Ealing Studios producer Michael Balcon joined forces with the British Film Institute to establish a scholarship fund in Vivien's name. The Vivien Leigh Award for Young Filmmakers—later known as the Vivien Leigh Memorial Fund—helped to fund the 1975 independent feature *Winstanley*, directed by Andrew Mollo and silent film historian and Acad-

Vivien pictured at Tickerage Mill not long before her death. Her ashes were later scattered on the millpond.

Angus McBean's photographs span the entire length of Vivien's career. These photos were taken during Vivien's final sitting with McBean in 1965.

emy Honorary Award winner Kevin Brownlow. In 1968 the biggest names in classic Hollywood cinema gathered at the University of Southern California to remember Vivien's "passionate devotion to her craft, a consuming quest for perfection, wide-ranging, achievement, and surpassing abilities of priceless individuality." The distinguished audience got "an added thrill" when George Cukor screened Vivien's tests from *Gone With the Wind* for the first time in thirty years. "I hadn't seen them myself since then," he told Gertrude Hartley. "They were electrifying. It was quite obvious why this accomplished, exciting, and beautiful creature got the part—it couldn't have been otherwise."

"Vivien was wonderful on the stage and on the screen," Alec Guinness said in 1991, "and if you can focus on the small shelf on which her volumes of effort rest, you really are staggered: Well, I am staggered at all that she accomplished in so short and selective a career and in so short a life." Today, Vivien's cinematic achievements remain her legacy. As John Kobal observed, "it took the camera to get to the heart of this woman, and make the need that drove this lovely, lonely spirit all the more appealing for asking nothing for itself except to be allowed to get on and do her work." In 1999, the

Dale McCarthy

Vivien's films remain her legacy. Her performance as Scarlett O'Hara continues to shine as one of most famous in Hollywood history.

American Film Institute named Vivien one of the twenty-five greatest actresses to have ever graced the silver screen. Compared to many of the other women on the list—Katharine Hepburn, Bette Davis, Joan Crawford, Barbara Stanwyck, Elizabeth Taylor—Vivien's filmography is small. Yet her contribution to cinematic culture was anything but.

Vivien believed that "truth is the keynote of all acting and of all artists." Her Scarlett O'Hara and Blanche DuBois—and many of her other perform-ances if we care to look closer—remain so powerful today because she revealed herself in each of these characters, and in doing so gave us a realistic glimpse into the human condition. When we watch Vivien on screen we often see our own reflection, not the cinematic fantasy of what we wish to be but what we truly are: flawed but unique human beings. What better evidence of a useful life?

Vivien fully embodied the glamor of her era
and is remembered today as a consummate star.

1935

Things Are Looking Up
Character: Schoolgirl (uncredited)
Director: Albert de Courville
Screenplay: Albert de Courville, Stafford Dickens
Also in the Cast: Cicely Courtneidge, Max Miller, William Gargan, Mary Lawson, Mark Lester
Producers: Michael Balcon, Alexander Korda for Gaumont British Picture Corporation

The Village Squire
Character: Rose Venables
Director: Reginald Denham
Screenplay: Sherard Powell, based on the play by Arthur Jarvis Black
Also in the Cast: David Horne, Leslie Perrins, Moira Lynd, Margaret Watson, Ivor Barnard
Producer: Anthony Havelock-Allan for British & Dominions Film Corporation

Gentleman's Agreement
Character: Phil Stanley
Director: George Pearson
Screenplay: Basil Mason, based on the story by Jennifer Howard
Also in the Cast: Frederick Peisley, Anthony Holles, David Horne, Vera Bogetti
Producer: Anthony Havelock-Allan for British & Dominions Film Corporation

Look Up and Laugh
Character: Marjorie Belfer
Director: Basil Dean
Screenplay: J. B. Priestly, Gordon Wellesley
Also in the Cast: Gracie Fields, Alfred Drayton, Douglas Wakefield, Billy Nelson, Harry Tate, Huntley Wright
Producer: Basil Dean for Associated Talking Pictures

1937

Fire Over England
Character: Cynthia
Director: William K. Howard
Screenplay: Clemence Dane, based on the novel by A. E. W. Mason
Also in the Cast: Flora Robson, Laurence Olivier, Leslie Banks, Raymond Massey, Tamara Desni
Producer: Alexander Korda for London Films

Dark Journey
Character: Madeleine Goddard
Director: Victor Saville
Screenplay: Lajos Bíró, Arthur Wimperis
Also in the Cast: Conrad Veidt, Joan Gardner, Anthony Bushell, Ursula Jeans
Producer: Alexander Korda for London Films

Storm in a Teacup
Character: Victoria Gow
Director: Victor Saville
Screenplay: Ian Dalrymple, Donald Bull, based on the play by James Bridie
Also in the Cast: Rex Harrison, Cecil Parker, Sara Allgood, Ursula Jeans
Producer: Alexander Korda for London Films

1938

A Yank at Oxford
Character: Elsa Craddock
Director: Jack Conway
Screenplay: John Monk Saunders, Leon Gordon
Also in the Cast: Robert Taylor, Lionel Barrymore, Maureen O'Sullivan, Edmund Gwenn, Griffith Jones
Producer: Michael Balcon for MGM

Sidewalks of London (St. Martin's Lane in the U.K.)
Character: Liberty "Libby"
Director: Tim Whelan
Screenplay: Bartlett Cormack, Clemence Dane, Charles Laughton, Erich Pommer, Tim Whelan
Also in the Cast: Charles Laughton, Rex Harrison, Larry Adler, Tyrone Guthrie
Producer: Erich Pommer and Charles Laughton for Mayflower Pictures Corp.

1939

Gone With the Wind
Character: Scarlett O'Hara
Director: Victor Fleming
Screenplay: Sidney Howard, based on the novel by Margaret Mitchell
Also in the Cast: Clark Gable, Leslie Howard, Olivia de Havilland, Hattie McDaniel, Thomas Mitchell
Producer: David O. Selznick for Selznick International

1940

Waterloo Bridge
Character: Myra Lester
Director: Mervyn LeRoy
Screenplay: S. N. Behrman, based on the play by Robert E. Sherwood
Also in the Cast: Robert Taylor, Virginia Field, Lucile Watson, Maria Ouspenskaya, C. Aubrey Smith
Producer: Sidney Franklin for MGM

21 Days Together (The First and the Last in the U.K.)
Character: Wanda
Director: Basil Dean
Screenplay: Basil Dean, Graham Greene, based on the story by John Galsworthy
Also in the Cast: Laurence Olivier, Leslie Banks, Francis L. Sullivan, David Horne, Robert Newton
Producer: Alexander Korda for London Films

1941

That Hamilton Woman (Lady Hamilton in the U.K.)
Character: Emma Hamilton
Director: Alexander Korda
Screenplay: Walter Reisch and R. C. Sherriff
Also in the Cast: Laurence Olivier, Sara Allgood, Henry Wilcoxon, Alan Mowbray, Gladys Cooper
Producer: Alexander Korda for London Films

1945

Caesar and Cleopatra
Character: Cleopatra
Director: Gabriel Pascal
Screenplay: George Bernard Shaw
Also in the Cast: Claude Raines, Stewart Granger, Flora Robson, Basil Sydney, Cecil Parker
Producer: J. Arthur Rank for the Rank Organization

1948

Anna Karenina
Character: Anna Karenina
Director: Julien Duvivier
Screenplay: Julien Duvivier, Jean Anouilh, Guy Morgan
Also in the Cast: Ralph Richardson, Kieron Moore, Sally Ann Howes, Hugh Dempster, Mary Kerridge
Producer: Alexander Korda for London Films

1951

A Streetcar Named Desire
Character: Blanche DuBois
Director: Elia Kazan
Screenplay: Tennessee Williams, Oscar Saul
Also in the Cast: Marlon Brando, Kim Hunter, Karl Malden, Rudy Bond, Nick Dennis
Producer: Charles K. Feldman

1955

The Deep Blue Sea
Character: Hester Collyer
Director: Anatole Litvak
Screenplay: Terence Rattigan, based on his play
Also in the Cast: Kenneth More, Moira Lister, Eric Portman, Emlyn Williams, Arthur Hill
Producer: Alexander Korda for London Films

1961

The Roman Spring of Mrs. Stone
Character: Karen Stone
Director: José Quintero
Screenplay: Gavin Lambert, based on the novel by Tennessee Williams
Also in the Cast: Warren Beatty, Lotte Lenya, Coral Browne, Jill St. John, Jeremy Spenser
Producer: Louis de Rochemont for Seven Arts Productions

1965

Ship of Fools
Character: Mary Treadwell
Director: Stanley Kramer
Screenplay: Abby Mann, based on the novel by Katherine Anne Porter
Also in the Cast: Lee Marvin, Simone Signoret, Oskar Werner, Elizabeth Ashley, José Ferrer, George Segal
Producer: Stanley Kramer for Stanley Kramer Productions

CHRONOLOGY OF PLAYS

1935

The Green Sash by Debonnaire Sylvester and T. P. Wood
Q Theatre, London
Character: Guista
Director: Matthew Forsyth

The Mask of Virtue by Carl Sternheim (adapted by Ashley Dukes)
Ambassadors Theatre, London
Character: Henriette Duquesnoy
Director: Maxwell Wray

1936

Richard III by William Shakespeare
Oxford University Dramatic Society
Character: The Queen
Directors: John Gielgud and Glen Byam Shaw

The Happy Hypocrite by Clemence Dane
His Majesty's Theatre, London
Character: Jenny Mere
Director: Maurice Colbourne

Henry VIII by William Shakespeare
Open Air Theatre, Regents Park, London
Character: Anne Boleyn
Director: Robert Atkins

1937

Because We Must by Ingaret Giffard
Wyndhams Theatre, London
Character: Pamela Golding-French
Director: Norman Marshall

Bats in the Belfry by Diana Morgan and Robert MacDermott
Ambassadors Theatre, London
Character: Jessica Morton
Director: A. R. Whatmore

Hamlet by William Shakespeare
Kronberg Castle, Denmark
Character: Ophelia
Director: Tyrone Guthrie

A Midsummer Night's Dream by William Shakespeare
Old Vic Theatre, London
Character: Tatiana
Director: Tyrone Guthrie

1938

Serena Blandish by S. N. Behrman
Gate Theatre, London
Character: Serena Blandish
Director: Esme Percy

1940

Romeo and Juliet by William Shakespeare
51st Street Theater, New York
Character: Juliet Capulet
Director: Laurence Olivier

1942

The Doctor's Dilemma by George Bernard Shaw
Theatre Royal Haymarket, London
Character: Jennifer Dubedat
Director: Irene Hentschel

1945*

The Skin of Our Teeth by Thornton Wilder
Phoenix Theatre, London
Character: Sabina
Director: Laurence Olivier
*Revived in 1946 at the Piccadilly Theatre, London

1948

Old Vic Tour of Australia and New Zealand, all opposite Laurence Olivier, who also directed:
Lady Anne in *Richard III*
Lady Teazle in *The School for Scandal*
Sabina in *The Skin of Our Teeth*

1949

New Theatre, London, for the Old Vic repertory season:
Lady Teazle in *The School for Scandal*
Lady Anne in *Richard III*
Antigone in *Antigone*

A Streetcar Named Desire by Tennessee Williams
Aldwych Theatre, London
Character: Blanche DuBois
Director: Laurence Olivier

1951

Caesar and Cleopatra* by George Bernard Shaw
St. James's Theatre, London
Character: Cleopatra
Director: Michael Benthall

Antony and Cleopatra* by William Shakespeare
> St. James's Theatre, London
> Character: Cleopatra
> Director: Michael Benthall
> *These two plays transferred to the Ziegfeld Theatre in New York in December 1951.

1953

The Sleeping Prince by Terence Rattigan
> Phoenix Theatre, London
> Character: Mary Morgan
> Director: Laurence Olivier

1955

Twelfth Night by William Shakespeare
> Shakespeare Memorial Theatre, Stratford-on-Avon
> Character: Viola
> Director: John Gielgud

Macbeth by William Shakespeare
> Shakespeare Memorial Theatre, Stratford-on-Avon
> Character: Lady Macbeth
> Director: Glen Byam Shaw

Titus Andronicus by William Shakespeare
> Shakespeare Memorial Theatre, Stratford-on-Avon
> Character: Lavinia
> Director: Peter Brook

1956

South Sea Bubble by Noel Coward
> Lyric Theatre, London
> Character: Lady Alexandra Shotter
> Director: William Chappell

1957

Titus Andronicus by William Shakespeare
> Stoll Theatre, London*
> Character: Lavinia
> Director: Peter Brook
> *Taken on tour in Paris, Vienna, Belgrade, Zagreb, and other parts of Europe for two months

1958

Duel of Angels by Jean Giraudoux (adapted by Christopher Fry)
> Apollo Theatre, London*
> Character: Paola
> Director: Jean-Louis Barrault
> *Re-staged in New York in 1960 under Robert Helpmann's direction

1959

Look After Lulu! by Noel Coward (based on Occupe-toi d'Amélie by Georges Feydeau)
> Royal Court Theatre, London
> Character: Lulu D'Arville
> Director: Tony Richardson

1960

Duel of Angels by Jean Giraudoux (adapted by Christopher Fry)
> Helen Hayes Theatre, New York (followed by three months tour of USA)
> Character: Paola
> Director: Robert Helpmann

1961

Old Vic Company tour of Australia, New Zealand, Mexico, and South America, directed by Roberto Helpmann:

Twelfth Night by William Shakespeare
> Character: Viola

Duel of Angels by Jean Giraudoux
> Character: Paola

Lady of the Camellias by Alexandre Dumas, fils
> Character: Marguerite Gautier

1963

Tovarich by Jacques Deval and Robert E. Sherwood
> Broadway Theatre, New York
> Character: Grand Duchess Tatiana I
> Director: Peter Glenville

1965

La Contessa by Paul Osborn
> English Provincial Tour, Newcastle, Liverpool, and Oxford
> Character: Contessa Sanziana
> Director: Robert Helpmann

1966

Ivanov by Anton Chekhov
> Schubert Theatre, New York
> Character: Anna Petrovna
> Director: John Gielgud

BIBLIOGRAPHY

Books

Bacall, Lauren. *By Myself and Then Some*. London: Headline, 2005.

Baer, William, ed. *Elia Kazan: Interviews*. Jackson: University of Mississippi Press, 2000.

Barker, Felix. *The Oliviers*. London: Hamish Hamilton, 1953.

Behlmer, Rudy, ed. *Memo From: David O. Selznick*. New York: The Viking Press, Inc., 1989.

Bloom, Claire. *Leaving a Doll's House*. London: Virago Press, 1996.

Braden, Bernard. *The Kindness of Strangers*. London: Hodder and Stoughton, 1990.

Brando, Marlon with Robert Lindsey. *Songs My Mother Taught Me*. London: Century, 1994.

Callow, Simon. *Charles Laughton: A Difficult Actor*. London: Methuen, 1987.

Chandler, Charlotte. *It's Only a Movie: Alfred Hitchcock: A Personal Biography*. New York: Simon & Schuster, 2005.

Clark, Kenneth. *The Other Half*. London: Hamish Hamilton, 1986.

Coleman, Terry. *Olivier*. London: Bloomsbury, 2005.

Costello, Donald P. *The Serpent's Eye: Shaw and the Cinema*. Indiana: University of Notre Dame Press

Coward, Noël. *The Letters of Noël Coward (Diaries, Letters, and Essays)*. Edited by Barry Day. London: Methuen Drama, 2008.

Dean, Basil. *Mind's Eye*. London: Hutchinson, 1973.

Deans, Marjorie. *Meeting at the Sphinx: Gabriel Pascal's Production of Bernard Shaw's Caesar and Cleopatra*. London: MacDonald and Co. Ltd., 1946.

Dent, Alan. *Vivien Leigh: A Bouquet*. London: Hamish Hamilton, 1969.

Drazin, Charles. *Korda: Britain's Movie Mogul*. London and New York: I. B. Tauris, 2002.

Edwards, Anne. *Vivien Leigh: A Biography*. New York: Simon & Schuster, 1977.

Finstad, Suzanne. *Warren Beatty: A Private Man*. New York: Harmony, 2005.

Forsyth, James. *Tyrone Guthrie: A Biography*. London: Hamish Hamilton, 1976.

Funke, Lewis and John E. Booth. *Actors Talk About Acting*. New York: Avon Book Division, 1961.

Godden, Jon and Rumer Godden. *Two Under the Indian Sun*. London: Beech Tree Books, 1987.

Granger, Stewart. *Sparks Fly Upward*. Great Britain: Granada Publishing Limited, 1981.

Gruen, John. *Close-up*. New York: The Viking Press, 1967.

Halsman, Philippe. *Sight and Insight*. New York: Doubleday, 1972.

Harris, Radie. *Radie's World*. London: W. H. Allen, 1975.

Harrison, Rex. *Rex*. London: Macmillan, 1974.

Holden, Anthony. *Laurence Olivier: A Biography*. London: Weidenfeld and Nicolson, 1988.

Howard, Jean. *Jean Howard's Hollywood: A Photo Memoir*. New York: Harry N. Abrams, Inc., 1989.

Huggett, Richard. *Binkie Beaumont: Eminence Grise of the West End Theatre, 1933–73*. London: Hodder & Stoughton, Ltd., 1989.

Kobal, John. *Hollywood Color Portraits*. New York: Morrow, 1981.

Kramer, Stanley with Thomas M. Coffey. *A Mad, Mad, Mad, Mad World: A Life in Hollywood*. London: Aurum Press, 1997.

Lambert, Gavin. *On Cukor*. New York: Rizzoli, 2000.

Lambert, Gavin. "Vivien Leigh: Internal Struggle." *In Close-ups: Intimate Profiles of Movie Stars by Their Co-stars, Directors, Screenwriters and Friends*. Edited by Danny Perry, 313–316. London: Windward, 1978.

Lasky, Jesse L. and Pat Silver. *Love Scene: The Story of Vivien Leigh and Laurence Olivier.* New York: Crowell, 1978.

Lejeune, Anthony, ed. *The C. A. Lejeune Film Reader.* Carcanet Press Ltd., 1991.

LeRoy, Mervyn and Dick Kleiner. *Mervyn LeRoy: Take One.* New York: Hawthorn Books, 1974.

Macqueen-Pope, W. *St. James's: Theatre of Distinction.* London: W. H. Allen, 1958.

Malden, Karl and Carla Malden. *When Do I Start?: A Memoir.* New York: Simon & Schuster, 1997.

Mangan, Richard, ed. *Gielgud Letters: John Gielgud in His Own Words.* London: Weidenfeld and Nicolson, 2004.

Marchant, William. *The Pleasure of His Company: Noël Coward Remembered.* London: Weidenfeld and Nicolson, 1975.

Mayer Selznick, Irene. *A Private View.* New York: Alfred A. Knopf, 1983.

McBean, Angus. *Vivien: A Love Affair in Camera.* London: Phaidon, 1990

Morgan, Michelle. *Marilyn Monroe: Private and Undisclosed.* London: Constable & Robinson, 2012.

Mullen, Michael, ed. *Macbeth Onstage: An Annotated Facsimile of Glen Byam Shaw's 1955 Promptbook.* Columbia & London: University of Missouri Press, 1976.

Niven, David. *Bring on the Empty Horses.* London: Hamish Hamilton, 1975.

Olivier, Laurence. *Confessions of an Actor.* London: Orion, 1982.

Olivier, Laurence. *On Acting.* London: Simon & Schuster, 1987.

Olivier, Tarquin. *My Father Laurence Olivier.* London: Headline Book Publishing, 1992.

Osborne, John. *Almost a Gentleman: An Autobiography Volume II 1955–1966.* London: Faber and Faber, 1991.

Payn, Graham and Sheridan Morley, eds. *The Noël Coward Diaries.* London: Da Capo Press, 2002.

Plowright, Joan. *And That's Not All.* London: Weidenfeld & Nicolson, 2001.

Ray, Bijoya. *Manik and I: My Life with Satyajit Ray.* London: Penguin UK, 2012.

Robyns, Gwen. *Light of a Star.* London: Leslie Frewen, 1968.

Russell Taylor, John. *Vivien Leigh.* London: Elm Tree Books, 1984.

Schickel, Richard. *Brando: A Life in Our Times.* London: Pavilion, 1991.

Shipman, David. *The Great Movie Stars: The Golden Years.* New York: Bonanza Books, 1972.

Signoret, Simone. *Nostalgia Isn't What It Used to Be.* New York: Harper & Row, 1978.

Staggs, Sam. *When Blanche Met Brando: The Scandalous Story of "A Streetcar Named Desire."* New York: St. Martin's Griffin, 2005.

Stockham, Martin. *The Korda Collection: Alexander Korda's Film Classics.* London: Boxtree Ltd., 1992.

Sweet, Matthew. *Shepperton Babylon: The Lost Worlds of British Cinema.* London: Faber and Faber Limited, 2005.

Thomson, David. *Showman: The Life of David O. Selznick.* New York: Alfred A. Knopf, 1992.

Thomson, David. *The New Biographical Dictionary of Film.* New York: Alfred A. Knopf, 2002.

Tierney, Gene with Mickey Herskowitz. *Self-Portrait.* New York: Wyden Books, 1979.

Tynan, Kathleen. *The Life of Kenneth Tynan.* London: Methuen, 1989.

Tynan, Kenneth. *He That Plays the King: A View of the Theatre.* London: Longmans, Green, 1950.

Vickers, Hugo. *Vivien Leigh.* London, New York, Toronto: Little, Brown and Company, 1988.

Victor, Adam. *The Marilyn Encyclopedia.* New York: The Overlook Press, 1999.

Vivienne with Anton Dolin. *They Came to My Studio: Famous People of Our Time.* London: Hall Productions, 1956.

Walker, Alexander. *Vivien: The Life of Vivien Leigh.* New York: Weidenfeld and Nicolson, 1987.

Williams, Tennessee. *A Streetcar Named Desire*. Edited by Michael Hooper and Patricia Hern. New York: A&C Black, 2009.

Williams, Tennessee. *Memoirs*. New York: Doubleday, 1975.

Windham, Donald, ed. *Tennessee Williams' Letters to Donald Windham 1940–1945*. New York: Holt, Reinhart and Winston, 1977.

Winn, Godfrey. *The Positive Hour*. Great Britain: Michael Joseph Ltd., 1970.

Pamphlets, Magazine, and Newspaper Articles

Agate, James. Review of *The Skin of Our Teeth*. *The Sunday Times*, May 18, 1945.

An Appreciation of Vivien Leigh: University of Southern California, March 17, 1968. University of Southern California: Friends of the Libraries, 1969.

Andersen, Christopher P. "Lord Olivier." *People*. January 10, 1963.

Berg, Louis. "Strictly Legitimate." *Los Angeles Times*. September 26, 1948.

Breen, Max. "Here Comes Vivien!" *The Picturegoer*. April 3, 1937.

Canfield, Alyce. "A Lady in Love." *Silver Screen*. January 1951.

Carroll, Roger. "The Woman Behind Scarlett." *Motion Picture*. February 1940.

Carson, James. "Don't Call me a Great Lover!." *Modern Screen*. June 1940.

Clayton, David. "Vivien is Back—With Vivacity." *Illustrated*. November 7, 1953.

Cook, Alton. Review of *The Deep Blue Sea*. *New York World Telegram*. October 12, 1955.

Daily Express. March 8, 1961.

Dent, Alan. "Vivien Leigh—The Star That Burned Too Bright." *News Chronicle*. March 21, 1953.

Evening Standard. September 14, 1946.

Gheman, Richard. "The Oliviers live their own love story." *Coronet*. January 1953.

Graham, Shiela. "Laurence Olivier made British lieutenant." *Washington Star*. August 17, 1941.

Hall, Rod. "Vivien Leigh: My Girl Next Door." *Mail on Sunday*. January 12, 2003.

Harcourt-Smith, Simon. Review of *Caesar and Cleopatra*. *The Tribune*. December 14, 1945.

Harris, Radie. "A Knight and His Lady." *Photoplay*. October 1946.

Haskell, Molly. "Real Love/Reel Love," *From the Current*, Criterion Collection. September 11, 2009.

Hill, Gladwin. "The Oliviers back in Hollywood." *The New York Times*. October 22, 1950.

Hinxman, Margaret. "The twenty questions everyone is asking about Vivien Leigh." *Picturegoer*. November 26, 1955.

Holman, Suzanne. "Vivien Leigh faces her biggest fight." *Sunday Chronicle*. March 22, 1953.

Hopper, Hedda. "Hedda Hopper's Hollywood." *Los Angeles Times*. January 16, 1939.

Hopper, Hedda. "Hedda Hopper's Hollywood." *Los Angeles Times*. December 18, 1939.

James, Paula. "Vivien Sobs as Love Story Ends." *Daily Mirror*. December 3, 1960.

Johns, Eric. "Vivien Leigh's World Tour." *Theatre World*. August, 1961.

Los Angeles Mirror, March 15, 1961.

Leff, Leonard J. "And Transfer to Cemetery: The Streetcars Named Desire." *Film Quarterly*. Spring 2002.

Leigh, Vivien. "I Gambled On a Musical," *Detroit Free Press*. Date unknown.

Leigh, Vivien. "*Tovarich* Isn't *Aida*." *The Philadelphia Enquirer Magazine*. January 13, 1963.

Leigh, Vivien. "Words, but if one of them were true?" *Theatre Illustrated Quarterly*. Summer 1935.

Lejeune, C. A. *The Observer*. December 12, 1945.

Linet, Beverly. "This is Vivien Leigh Today." *Modern Screen*. September 1960.

Lewin, David. "Vivien Tells." *The Daily Express*. August 17, 1960.

Newham, John K. "Vivien Leigh's Strange Career." *Film Weekly*. April 3, 1937.

Newsweek. February 2, 1947.

Newsweek. June 6, 1960.

The New York Times. March 20, 1963.

Nugent, Frank S. "Gone With the Wind (1939)." *The New York Times*. December 20, 1939.

"Oliviers Quit Hotel To Escape Curious Crowd." *Sydney Morning Herald*. June 22, 1948.

Ottaway, Robert. "Vivien Leigh: The Mask Behind the Face." March 10, 1965.

Parsons, Harriet. "Will Vivien Leigh be Gone with the Wind?" *Los Angeles Examiner*. 1940.

Parsons, Louella. "Louella O. Parsons in Hollywood," *Los Angeles Examiner*, April 19, 1953.

Pictorial Review. October 22, 1950.

"Polish Up an Oscar," *Holiday*. October 1951.

Rattigan, Terence. *The New York Times*. August 6, 1967.

Reeve, Elizabeth. "The Old Vic on tour: An appraisal." Publication unknown. Autumn-Winter 1962.

Roosevelt, Eleanor. "My Day." United States Feature Syndicate. May 3, 1948.

Robinson, Wayne. "'Tovarich' Premieres Tomorrow." *Philadelphia Sunday Bulletin*. January 20, 1963.

"Rudolf Karl Freudenberg." *Psychiatric Bulletin*. 1983, 7:215.

Scheuer, Philip K. "Vivien Leigh Returns South in 'Streetcar.'" *Los Angeles Times*. August 1950.

Schier, Ernest. "Vivien Leigh: What is Undone Will Be Done." *Philadelphia Sunday Bulletin*. March 13, 1966.

"Sir Laurence Olivier 'Asks for Divorce." *Times* (London). May 23, 1960.

"Streetcar." *The New York Times*. August 21, 1950

The Age (Melbourne). April 21, 1948.

The Billboard. December 30, 1939.

The Guardian. July 10, 1967.

The Mail (Adelaide). April 17, 1948.

The Observer. July 9, 1967.

TIME. July 22, 1957.

Times (London). May 9, 1963.

Truth (Christchurch). October 1948.

Tynan, Kenneth. *The Observer*. June 12, 1955.

Underhill, Duncan. "Vivien Meets her Waterloo." *Screen Life*. May, 1940.

"Vivien Leigh Says Aust. Tour 'too heavy." *The Mail* (Adelaide). May 21, 1949.

"Vivien Leigh Wears Molyneaux." *British Vogue*. June 1941.

Winn, Godfrey. "Godfrey Winn talks with his dear friend Vivien Leigh." *Woman*. September 26, 1964.

Woolf, S. J. "Juliet, Not Scarlett." *The New York Times*. June 9, 1940.

Documentaries and Televised Interviews

60 Minutes interview with Laurence Olivier (CBS, 1983)

Cinema with Michael Parkinson (Granada, 1969)

Great Acting: Laurence Olivier (BBC, 1966)

Larry and Vivien: The Oliviers in Love (Channel 4, 2001)

Living Famously: Vivien Leigh (BBC, 2003)

Our World: The Making of Gone With the Wind (ABC, 1987)

Small World with Edward R. Murrow (CBS, December 1958)

Vivien Leigh: Scarlett and Beyond (Turner Entertainment, 1990)

CHAPTER NOTES

Introduction

We have to love: Sir Alec Guinness, interview with James Grissom, 1991.

a Queen who requires: *Evening Standard*, September 14, 1946.

I hope my life: Vivien Leigh, letter to Laurence Olivier, June 20 1960. Olivier Archive, British Library (London).

Chapter 1: Fame in a Night

That's the man: David Lewin, "Vivien Tells," *The Daily Express*, August 17, 1960.

(caption) *I like dressing up*: Lewis Funke and John E. Booth, *Actors Talk About Acting* (New York: Avon Book Division, 1961), 78.

She was always: Maureen O'Sullivan, voiceover on *Living Famously: Vivien Leigh* (BBC, 2003).

Later in life: Joan Plowright, *And That's Not All* (London: Weidenfeld & Nicolson, 2001), 61.

dark Eastern beauty: Hugo Vickers, *Vivien Leigh* (London, New York, Toronto: Little, Brown and Company, 1988), 6.

the determined one: Lewin, "Vivien Tells."

a bewitching little girl: John and Rumer Godden, *Two Under the Indian Sun* (London: Beech Tree Books, 1987), 161.

knew things were bad: Jack

Merivale, recorded memo for Anne Edwards, box 35, collection 1080, Anne Edwards Papers, UCLA (Los Angeles).

a sort-of kicking board: Hester St. John-Ives, interview with author, January 24, 2013.

there was an air: Alan Dent, *Vivien Leigh: A Bouquet*, (London: Hamish Hamilton, 1969), 46.

I can see her now: ibid.

Cossetted and pampered by the nuns: ibid, 48.

grown up: ibid, 44.

She said it would: ibid, 43.

so disappointed at: ibid.

Brigit Boland, the child producer: Vickers, *Vivien Leigh*, 16.

That was one of the things: Roger Carroll, "The Woman Behind Scarlett," *Motion Picture*, February 1940.

. . . In fact, all: Funke and Booth, *Actors Talk About Acting*, 80.

I was not: Vickers, *Vivien Leigh*, 38.

thought that she: *Larry and Vivien: The Oliviers in Love* (Channel 4, 2001).

so uncontrollably nervous: Basil Dean, *Mind's Eye* (London: Hutchinson, 1973), 207.

Don't worry, love: Felix Barker, *The Oliviers* (London: Hamish Hamilton, 1953), 94.

I remember the morning: Funke and Booth, *Actors talk About Acting*, 82.

Every night I play: Vivien Leigh, "Words, But if One of Them Were True?" *Theatre Illustrated Quarterly*, Summer 1935.

which she did: Charles Drazin, *Korda: Britain's Movie Mogul* (London and New York: I.B. Tauris, 2002), 161.

One final word: Leigh, "Words, But if One of Them Were True?"

Except for seeing: Christopher P. Andersen, "Lord Olivier," *People*, January 10, 1983.

I was very indignant: Lewin, "Vivien Tells."

We shall probably: Barker, *The Oliviers*, 111.

I wonder whether: Godfrey Winn, *The Positive Hour* (Great Britain: Michael Joseph Ltd., 1970), 397.

Rubbish, I don't know: Max Breen, "Here Comes Vivien!" *The Picturegoer*, April 3, 1937.

very frightening father figure: Laurence Olivier, interview with Kenneth Tynan, *Great Acting* (BBC, 1966).

the most important recruit: Breen, "Here Comes Vivien!"

Their joyous awareness: Dean, *Mind's Eye*, 251.

bustle in and kiss her: Matthew Sweet, *Shepperton Babylon: The Lost Worlds of British Cinema*

(London: Faber and Faber Limited, 2005), 143.

a mixture of: Barker, *The Oliviers*, 125.

most of what: ibid.

Vivien L. who: Unknown author, letter written June 1937, collection of Richard Mangan.

. . . She contains within her: Simon Callow, *Charles Laughton: A Difficult Actor* (London: Methuen, 1987), 127.

never so much as: Rex Harrison, *Rex* (London: Macmillan, 1974), 52.

disappear into her dressing room: Alexander Walker, *Vivien: The Life of Vivien Leigh* (New York: Weidenfeld and Nicholson, 1987), 104.

Expelled his own wife: ibid, 103.

Chapter 2: Scarlett

Scarlett was a: Carroll, "The Woman Behind Scarlett."

a girl who: Russell Birdwell, Selznick International Press Release for *Gone With the Wind*, January 1939.

The public wanted: Evelyn Keyes, interviewed on *Vivien Leigh: Scarlett and Beyond* (Turner Pictures, 1990).

Everyone said I: Lewin, "Vivien Tells."

The conversation came: Anthony Lejeune, ed., *The C. A. Lejeune Film Reader* (Carcanet Press Ltd., 1991), 34–35.

I'll play Cathy: William Wyler, interviewed on *Vivien Leigh: Scarlett and Beyond* (Turner Pictures, 1990).

I said to her: ibid.

Naturally, I'm the only: David Thomson, *Showman: The Life of David O. Selznick* (New York: Knopf Doubleday, 1992), 286.

Long contracts are: "Vivien Leigh: Adorable Vixen," *News Review*, February 10, 1949.

One can hardly: Hedda Hopper, "Hedda Hopper's Hollywood," *Los Angeles Times*, January 16, 1939.

In her physical: Birdwell, Selznick International Press Release for *Gone With the Wind*.

She is five: ibid.

It is difficult, really: Paul Harrison, "Vivien Leigh admits she doesn't like movies much," June 1939.

Playing Rhett Butler: Olivia de Havilland, interview with author, January 28, 2013.

Gable was always: Marcella Rabwin, interviewed for "Making Gone With the Wind," *Our World* (ABC, 1988).

lacked the big: Rudy Behlmer, ed., *Memo From: David O. Selznick* (New York: The Viking Press, Inc., 1989), 192.

Ham it up: Anne Edwards, *Vivien Leigh: A Biography* (New York: Simon & Schuster, 1977), 101.

One day she: Gavin Lambert, *On Cukor* (New York: Rizzoli, 2000), 149.

stick that script: Edwards, *Vivien Leigh*, 101.

embittered, tougher, bitchier: David Thomson, *Showman: The Life of David O. Selznick*, p. 296.

Vivien was very: Olivia de Havilland, interview with author, January 28, 2013.

Poor little Vivien: Sunny Lash, letter to Laurence Olivier, June 20, 1960, Olivier Archive, British Library (London).

On April 17: Thomson, Showman: *The Life of David O. Selznick*, 298.

I'm afraid you: Terry Coleman, *Olivier*, p. 127.

Each night after: Sunny Lash, letter to Laurence Olivier, June 20, 1960.

All I'm conscious: Carroll, "The Woman Behind Scarlett."

This was a woman: Irene Mayer Selznick, *A Private View* (New York: Alfred A. Knopf, 1983), 223.

Vivien Leigh was: Charlotte Chandler, *It's Only a Movie: Alfred Hitchcock: A Personal Biography*, (New York: Simon & Schuster, 2005), 10.

I'd like to: Carroll, "The Woman Behind Scarlett."

in a blaze: *The Billboard*, December 30, 1939.

crowds larger than: "G With the W," *TIME*, December 25, 1939.

Ladies and gentlemen: Hearst Movietone Newsreel footage of *Gone With the Wind* premiere, December 1939.

Miss Leigh's Scarlett: Frank S. Nugent, "Gone With the Wind (1939)", *The New York Times*, December 20, 1939.

Now, by golly: Hedda Hopper, "Hedda Hopper's Hollywood," *Los Angeles Times*, December 18, 1939.

Will Vivien Leigh: Harriet Parsons, "Will Vivien Leigh Be Gone with the Wind?" *Los Angeles Examiner*, 1940.

After Gone With the Wind: Barker, *The Oliviers*, 166-167.

Chapter 3: The War Years

I really feel: Sheilah Graham, "Laurence Olivier made British lieutenant," *Washington Star*, August 17, 1941.

always said it: Mervyn LeRoy and Dick Kleiner, *Mervyn LeRoy: Take One* (New York: Hawthorn Books, 1974), 146.

classic piece of: Vickers, *Vivien Leigh*, 120.

I'm afraid it: ibid.

A day's work: Duncan Underhill, "Vivien Meets her Waterloo," *Screen Life*, May 1940.

Everything seems so: S. J. Woolf, "Juliet, Not Scarlett," *The New York Times*, June 9, 1940.

Theirs was certainly: Olivia de Havilland, interview with author, January 28, 2013.

Miss Leigh has: James Carson, "Don't Call me a Great Lover!," *Modern Screen*, June 1940.

Last week one: Review of *Romeo and Juliet*, TIME, May 1940.

The audience had: Robert Ottaway, "Vivien Leigh: The Mask Behind the Face," March 10, 1965.

Jumped up little movie stars: Radie Harris, *Radie's World* (London: W. H. Allen, 1975), 166.

the production went down: ibid.

When I made: Lewin, "Vivien Tells."

I wired you: Vickers, *Vivien Leigh*, 127.

I really didn't know: Alexander Walker, *Vivien: The Life of Vivien Leigh* (New York: Weidenfeld and Nicolson, 1987), 150.

encapsulates the eternal: Molly Haskell, "That Hamilton Woman: Real Love/Reel Love," *From the Current*, Criterion Collection, September 11, 2009.

cardboard hero required: Anthony Holden, *Olivier: A Biography* (London: Weidenfeld and Nicolson, 1988), 165.

give full reign: Haskell, "That Hamilton Woman: Real Love/Reel Love."

The audience would: James Forsyth, *Tyrone Guthrie: A Biography* (London: Hamish Hamilton, 1976), 183.

a terribly affected creature: Funke and Booth, *Actors Talk About Acting*, 87.

Glad to be back: "Vivien Leigh wears Molyneaux," *British Vogue*, June 1941.

At first I went: Kenneth Clark, *The Other Half* (London: Hamish Hamilton, 1986), 60.

Vivien is almost incredibly: Vickers, *Vivien Leigh*, 137.

Giving pleasure to: Richard Huggett, *Binkie Beaumont: Eminence Grise of the West End Theatre, 1933–73* (London: Hodder & Stoughton, Ltd., 1989), 281.

Because of dangerous: Vivien Leigh, letter to Laurence Olivier, July 15, 1943, Olivier Archive, British Library (London).

. . . I felt so: Vivien Leigh, letter to Laurence Olivier, June 22, 1943, Olivier Archive, British Library (London).

It is a curious: Marjorie Deans, *Gabriel Pascal's Production of Bernard Shaw's Caesar and Cleopatra* (London: MacDonald and Co. Ltd., 1946), 65.

Script supervisor Marjorie: Ibid, 89.

Christ, it's old Jim: Stewart Granger, *Sparks Fly Upward* (Great Britain: Granada Publishing Limited, 1981), 85.

What do you suppose: Vickers, *Vivien Leigh*, 156.

Didn't care for: Jesse L. Lasky and Pat Silver, *Love Scene: The Story of Vivien Leigh and Laurence Olivier* (New York: Crowell, 1978), 89.

Everyone is very: Vickers, *Vivien*

Leigh, 156.

hurry up and: Ibid.

It is, let's face it: Simon Harcourt-Smith, *The Tribune*, December 14, 1945.

a singularly cold triumph: C. A. Lejeune, *The Observer*, December 12, 1945.

Soon after rehearsals: Barker, *The Oliviers*, 224.

Through it all: James Agate, *The Sunday Times*, May 18, 1945.

Your sorrow is my: Coleman, *Olivier*, 180.

Hearing word of her illness: David O. Selznick, letter to Vivien Leigh, August 1945, Olivier Archive, British Library (London).

Chapter 4: Theater Royalty

Her name, combined: The Guardian, July 10, 1967.

Imagine life without: Tarquin Olivier, *My Father Laurence Olivier* (London: Headline Book Publishing, 1992), 235-36.

Renee Asherson, who: Renee Asherson, interview with author, June 10, 2012.

were precisely the things: Olivier, *My Father Laurence Olivier*, 136.

And the artists: Lewin, "Vivien Tells."

In February 1946: Letter from Laurence Olivier to Stephen Watts, February 1946, Olivier Archive, British Library (London).

I never saw: Alec Guinness, interview with James Grissom, 1991.

There's nothing my: Funke and Booth, *Actors Talk About Acting*, 85.

I'm told that Darryl Zanuck: Radie Harris, "A Knight and His Lady," *Photoplay*, October 1946.

exquisite, she was full: Philippe Halsman, *Sight and Insight* (New York: Doubleday, 1972), 139.

You won't take it: Coleman, *Olivier*, 196.

The leading lady: Vickers, *Vivien Leigh*, 174.

So poorly miscast: Newsweek, February 2, 1947.

What do you think: Olivier, *My Father Laurence Olivier*, 147.

I know about Anna: Vickers, *Vivien Leigh*, 176.

No one can top Garbo: Louis Berg, "Strictly legitimate," *Los Angeles Times*, September 26, 1948.

could act love: Terence Rattigan, *The New York Times*, August 16, 1967.

One hundred percent: Martin Stockham, The Korda Collection: *Alexander Korda's Film Classics* (London: Boxtree Ltd., 1992), 126.

When I was a little girl: Lewin, "Vivien Tells."

An attitude circulated: Gwen Robyns, *Light of a Star* (London: Leslie Frewen, 1968), 114.

We all thought it was: Michael Blakemore, interviewed for *Larry and Vivien: The Oliviers in Love*.

Her dedication was: The Mail, Adelaide, April 17, 1948.

It was worth: The Age, Melbourne, April 21, 1948

The show attracted: Ibid.

A first gentleman and lady: Truth, Christchurch, October 1948.

In answer to a question: The Age, Melbourne, April 20, 1948.

There's never been anything: Michael Redington, interview on ABC's Radio National, Australia, September 3, 2011.

Shocking state of affairs: Sydney Morning Herald, June 29, 1948.

If we don't have peace: Sydney Morning Herald, June 22, 1948.

You may not know it: Quoted in Holden, *Olivier: A Biography*, 243.

Why, we saw practically nothing: The Mail, Adelaide, May 21, 1949.

Something had cooled: Georgina Jumel, interview for *Larry and Vivien: The Oliviers in Love*.

It had always been inconceivable: Laurence Olivier, *Confessions of an Actor* (London: Weidenfeld and Nicolson, 1982), 172.

Pathological obsession: Psychiatric report by Dr. Arthur Conachy, June 20, 1961, Jack

Merivale Papers, BFI Library (London).

Chapter 5: Streetcar

Vivien's Blanche: was certainly: Dent, Vivien Leigh: A Bouquet, 103.

Vivien Leigh is not really: Donald Windham, ed., Tennessee Williams's *Letters to Donald Windham 1940–1945* (Athens: University of Georgia Press, 1996), 241.

Vivien centered the whole: Tennessee Williams, *Memoirs* (New York: Doubleday, 1975), 266.

He said, 'Oh, the': Mayer Selznick, *A Private View*, 325.

However, a lengthy letter: Copy of letter from Laurence Olivier to Tennessee Williams, September 1949, Olivier Archive, British Library (London).

Everyone said I was mad: Lewin, "Vivien Tells."

If the critics lead: Bernard Braden, *The Kindness of Strangers* (London: Hodder and Stoughton, 1990), 87.

Olivier bluntly told Williams: Copy of Letter from Laurence Olivier to Tennessee Williams, September 1949.

When he gave her a direction: Braden, *The Kindness of Strangers*, 67.

Showing such signs: Copy of Letter from Laurence Olivier to Tennessee Williams, September 1949.

English people perhaps are: Lewin, "Vivien Tells."

Noël Coward went to see: Graham Payn and Sheridan Morely, eds. *The Noël Coward Diaries* (London: Da Capo Press, 2002), 134.

The audiences who come and: Richard Mangan, ed. Gielgud *Letters: John Gielgud in His Own Words* (London: Weidenfeld and Nicholson, 2004), 127.

Arrange it to suit Gracie: Braden, *The Kindness of Strangers*, 135.

One of the most romantic: Pictorial Review, October 22, 1950.

People were almost threatening: Vickers, *Vivien Leigh*, 200.

There was never a more romantic: Jean Howard, *Jean Howard's Hollywood: A Photo Memoir* (New York: Harry N. Abrams, Inc., 1989), 112.

Some things have to be: Gladwin Hill, "The Oliviers back in Hollywood," *The New York Times*, October 22, 1950.

I could not share: Lewin, "Vivien tells."

When she came over here: William Baer, ed. *Elia Kazan: Interviews*. (Jackson: University of Mississippi Press, 2000), 134-35.

She doesn't care how: Alyce Canfield, "A Lady in Love," *Silver Screen*, January 1951.

Actual beauty— beauty of feature: Funke and Booth, *Actors Talk About Acting*, 83.

had a small talent: Richard Schickel, *Brando: A Life in Our Times* (London: Pavilion, 1991), 64.

I had nine months in: Quoted in *Coleman*, Olivier, 236.

break in Vivien: Sam Staggs, *When Blanche Met Brando: The Scandalous Story of "A Streetcar Named Desire"* (New York: St. Martin's Griffin, 2005), 167.

I had no sense of it: Kim Hunter, interviewed for *Vivien Leigh: Scarlett and Beyond* (Turner Pictures, 1990).

In many ways she: Marlon Brando with Robert Lindsey, *Songs My Mother Taught Me* (London: Century, 1994), 150.

Why do you have to: Lewin, "Vivien tells."

Finally ended up sitting: Karl Malden and Carla Malden, *When Do I Start?: A Memoir* (New York: Simon & Schuster, 1997), 192–93.

Only twice, you know: Vivien Leigh, interviewed for *Small World* with Edward R. Murrow, (CBS, December 1958).

In the 1950s: was a hell of a lot better: Baer, *Elia Kazan: Interviews*, 135.

England's great Vivien Leigh: Bosley Crowther, *The New York Times*, September 20, 1951.

Polish up an Oscar: Holiday, October 1951.

It is possible not to be: David Shipman, *The Great Movie Stars: The Golden Years* (New York: Bonanza Books, 1972), 339.

In The New Biographical: David Thomson, *The New Biographical Dictionary of Film* (New York: Alfred A. Knopf, 2002), 509.

I've read Stanislavsky: Funke and Booth, *Actors talk About Acting*, 79.

Chapter 6: Between the Devil and the Deep Blue Sea

Vivien was beautiful: Alec Guinness, interview with James Grissom, 1991.

I have always tried to tackle: "Vivien—The Happiness and the Heartache," *Sunday Mirror*, July 7, 1967.

She was brilliant: Laurence Olivier, *On Acting* (London: Simon & Schuster, 1987), 117.

Vivien and I were set: Ibid.

if not angry: Edward R. Murrow, *Small World* (CBS, December 1958).

a posturing butterfly: Kenneth Tynan, *He That Plays the King: A View of the Theatre* (London: Longmans, Green, 1950), 94.

Put Vivien Leigh into her: Kathleen Tynan, *The Life of Kenneth Tynan* (London: Methuen, 1989), 94.

Overpraise, in the end: Ibid.

the only young actress: *Evening Standard*, September 14, 1946.

Should we be too tired: Olivier, *Confessions of an Actor*, 184.

so ill that she would: Dent, *Vivien Leigh: A Bouquet*, 73.

Actors are shy people: Lewin, "Vivien Tells."

An official verdict came: Psychiatric report by Dr. Arthur Conachy, June 20, 1961.

Larry is worried about Vivien: Payn and Morely, *Noël Coward Diaries*, 191.

With the knell of: Olivier, *Confessions of an Actor*, 196.

Like a thing—an amoeba: Lewin, "Vivien Tells."

Marked elevation of mood: Psychiatric report by Dr. Arthur Conachy, June 20, 1961.

She wrote of a sudden impulse: Vivien Leigh, telegrams to Laurence Olivier, January 30 and January 31, 1953, Olivier Archive, British Library (London).

Aware that he was coming: Vivien Leigh, telegram to Laurence Olivier, February 6, 1953, Olivier Archive, British Library (London).

all the luck he needed: Olivier, *Confessions of an Actor*, 197.

despite a reminder from Olivier: Telegram from Laurence Olivier to Vivien Leigh, February 26, 1953, Olivier Archive, British Library (London).

I can't always be: Untitled article, *Screen Fan*, July 1953, clippings files, Margaret Herrick Library (Beverly Hills).

I think this will be my: Louella Parsons, "Louella O. Parsons in Hollywood," *Los Angeles Examiner*, April 19, 1953.

Enjoyed tearing up money: Vickers, *Vivien Leigh*, 213.

Dr. Barney Kully: Irving Asher, telegram to Laurence Olivier, March 6, 1953, Olivier Archive, British Library (London).

Occasionally she would let out: David Niven, *Bring on the Empty Horses* (London: Hamish Hamilton, 1975), 484.

In the early hours: Itemized invoice from Dr. Fraser McDonald to Laurence Olivier Productions for services relating to care of Vivien Leigh, March 31, 1953, Olivier Archive, British Library (London).

He lovingly cabled: Laurence Olivier, telegram to Vivien Leigh, March 6, 1953, Olivier Archive, British Library (London).

Her eyes were misted: Olivier, *Confessions of an Actor*, 201.

In Hollywood, Vivien was: Ibid.

When my time came: Gene Tierney with Mickey Herskowitz, *Self-Portrait* (New York: Wyden Books, 1979), 210.

Instead, Olivier spent a total: Itemized statement for seven days psychiatric care in Hollywood, sent to Cecil Tennant from Dr. Ralph R. Greenson, March 31 1953, Olivier Archive, British Library (London).

The Los Angeles Times reported: Los Angeles Times, March 19, 1953.

Biting and scratching: Olivier, *Confessions of an Actor*, 203.

Getting her home was: Olivier, *My Father Laurence Olivier*, 173.

After the Second World War: Eleanor Roosevelt, "My Day," United States Feature Syndicate, May 3, 1948.

Warm and humorous: Obituary for Rudolf Karl Freudenberg, *Psychiatric Bulletin*, 1983, 7:215.

Burn marks on her temples: Tarquin Olivier, interviewed for *Larry and Vivien: The Oliviers in Love*.

During one course: Unpublished draft for Laurence Olivier's auto-biography, *Confessions of An Actor*, Olivier Archive, British Library (London).

The treatment was progressing: Dr. Rudolf Freudenberg, letter to Laurence Olivier, March 29, 1953, Olivier Archive, British Library (London).

On April 5, he found: Ibid. April 5, 1953.

Some suggested specialists: Letters of condolence from Vivien's fans to Laurence Olivier concerning Vivien's breakdown in 1953, Olivier Archive, British Library (London)

Well, dear, gracious: Alan Dent, "Vivien Leigh: The star that has burned too bright," *News Chronicle*, March 21, 1953.

Next Tuesday evening: Suzanne Holman, "Vivien Leigh faces her biggest fight," *Sunday Chronicle*, March 22, 1953.

solemnly promised to be: Payn and Morely, *Noël Coward Diaries*, 211.

Chapter 7: The End of the Affair

There are two things: Richard Gheman, "The Oliviers live their own love story," *Coronet*, January 1953.

All the old liveliness: David Clayton, "Vivien is Back—With Vivacity," *Illustrated*, November 7, 1953.

bewitching in the piece: Olivier, *My Father Laurence Olivier*, 177.

Vivien "wanted glamour": Dent, *Vivien Leigh: A Bouquet*, 82.

second only to George: Howard, *Jean Howard's Hollywood*, 205.

a fine director: Margaret Hinxman, "The twenty questions everyone is asking about Vivien Leigh," *Picturegoer*, November 26, 1955.

He had this theory: Vickers, *Vivien Leigh*, 220.

one of her most brilliant: Alton Cook, *New York World Telegram*, October 12, 1955.

No amount of sheer integrity: Dent, *Vivien Leigh: A Bouquet*, 132.

Tears came into her eyes: Vickers, *Vivien Leigh*, 229.

I'm never satisfied: Hinxman, "The twenty questions everyone is asking about Vivien Leigh."

One of the best Macbeths: Michael Mullen, ed. *Macbeth Onstage: An Annotated Facsimile of Glen Byam Shaw's 1955 Promptbook* (Columbia & London: University of Missouri Press, 1976), 10.

She lowered her voice: Ibid, 251.

When John Clements took over: Jack Merivale, recorded memo for Anne Edwards, Anne Edwards Papers, UCLA (Los Angeles).

I always used to worry: Lewin, "Vivien Tells."

In a 1983 interview: Laurence Olivier, interview with Kathleen Tynan, British Library Theatre Archive Project, August 4 and 16, 1983.

To Ken, Vivien was: Ibid.

worst errors of judgment: John Russell Taylor, *Vivien Leigh* (London: Elm Tree Books, 1984), 99.

She should develop along: Payn and Morely, *Noël Coward Diaries*, 279.

as if she had lost: Olivier, *Confessions of an Actor*, 216.

in a very bad way: Richard Mangan, ed., *Gielgud Letters: John Gielgud in His Own Words* (London: Weidenfeld and Nicolson, 2004), 188.

She recounted an amusing story: William Marchant, *The Pleasure of His Company: Noël Coward Remembered* (London: Weidenfeld and Nicolson, 1975), 105–110.

Oh, you know men: Coleman, *Olivier*, 282.

she certainly wouldn't want: Hester St. John-Ives, interview with author, January 24, 2013.

I thought, heaven help me: Lewin, "Vivien Tells."

a model, not an actress: Laurence Olivier, interviewed for *Cinema* with Michael Parkinson (Granada, 1969).

Nearly thirty years would pass: Adam Victor, *The Marilyn Encyclopedia* (New York: The Overlook Press, 1999), 227.

According to biographer Adam Victor: Ibid, 189.

The British public would never accept: John Osborne, *Almost a Gentleman: An Autobiography Volume II 1955–1966* (London: Faber and Faber, 1991), 37.

None of us likes to admit: Vivien Leigh, foreword to *St. James's: Theatre of Distinction*, by W. Macqueen-Pope (London: W.H. Allen, 1958), 9-10.

Simply an obsolete: *TIME*, July 22, 1957.

People were overjoyed: Fan letters to Vivien Leigh praising her efforts to save the St. James's Theatre, Olivier Archive, British Library (London).

England would be all: Enid Fearney, letter to Vivien Leigh, July 1957, Olivier Archive, British Library (London).

She failed but: W. Macqueen-Pope, *St. James's: Theatre of Distinction*, 216.

trapped by public acclaim: Payn and Morely, *Noël Coward Diaries*, 278.

She did not willingly seek: Laurence Olivier, letter to Hester St. John-Ives, February 17, 1959.

There was even a story: Colin Clark, interviewed for *Larry and Vivien: The Oliviers in Love.*

People were passed out: Hester St. John-Ives, interview with author, January 24, 2013.

An almost unbroken: Osborne, *Almost a Gentleman*, 134.

Vivien was really lucky: Hester St. John-Ives, interview with author, January 24, 2013.

a better stage actress: Claire Bloom, interview with author, March 18, 2012.

Viven's virtue, always a: Osborne, *Almost a Gentleman*, 135.

I have come to the conclusion: Vivien Leigh, letter to Laurence Olivier, November 3, 1958, Olivier Archive, British Library, London.

The marriage had been heaven: Lauren Bacall, *By Myself and Then Some* (London: Headline, 2005), 327.

My heart aches: Laurence Olivier, letter to Hester St. John-Ives, February 1959.

I said, "I'm sorry": Laurence Olivier, interviewed for *60 Minutes* (CBS News, 1983).

because it was expedient: Lewin, "Vivien Tells."

making Christmas & the New Year: Vivien Leigh, letter to Noël Coward, January 1960, Noël Coward Foundation (London).

Vivien, with deep sadness: Payn and Morely, *Noël Coward Diaries*, 427.

It has been a most wretched: Olivier, *My Father Laurence Olivier*, 235.

Chapter 8: Twilight

I know everyone has to face: Godfrey Winn, "Godfrey Winn talks with his dear friend Vivien Leigh," *Woman*, September 26, 1964.

eternal and unchanging: Winn, *The Positive Hour*, 384.

The tabloid Daily Mirror: Paula James, "Vivien Sobs as Love Story Ends," *Daily Mirror*, December 3, 1960.

Whatever happens let us be friends: Vivien Leigh, letter to Laurence Olivier, June 20, 1960, Olivier Archive, British Library, London.

really believed that he: Hester St. John-Ives, interview with author, January 24, 2013.

At Eaton square: Coleman, *Olivier*, 332.

He gave her every reason: Hester St. John-Ives, interview with author, June 20, 2013.

It was a can of pears: Louise Olivier, *interview with author*, September 19, 2012.

I shall never marry again: Winn, *The Positive Hour*, 397.

Any ass who can't: Newsweek, June 6, 1960.

We've been together for: Edwards, *Vivien Leigh*, 123.

It really wasn't until: Jack Merivale, recorded memo for Anne Edwards, box 35, collection 1080, Anne Edwards Papers, UCLA (Los Angeles).

felt that it was intended: Plowright: *And That's Not All*, 74.

didn't feel this was any time: Ibid, 77.

She was very tough with him: John Gielgud, interviewed for *Vivien Leigh: Scarlett and Beyond* (Turner Pictures, 1990).

No one could ever know: Jack Merivale, recorded memo for Anne Edwards, box 35, collection 1080, Anne Edwards Papers, UCLA (Los Angeles).

Then, one day Tennessee said: Gavin Lambert, "Vivien Leigh: Internal Struggle," in *Close-ups: Intimate Profiles of Movie Stars by their Co-stars, Directors, Screenwriters and Friends*, ed. Danny Perry (London: Windward, 1978), 313.

grace and dignity to a role: TIME, December 29, 1961.

No one can sit on a banquet: Bosley Crowther, *The New York Times*, December 29, 1961.

The beginning of: Hollywood Citizen-News, December 30, 1961.

I was a great fan: Jill St. John, interviewed for *The Roman Spring of Mrs. Stone: Looking for Light in All the Dark Corners* (Sparkhill Productions, 2006).

One could not help: Olivia de Havilland, interview with author, January 29, 2013.

The picture has been released: Los Angeles Mirror, March 15, 1961.

Twenty-one years!: Daily Express, March 8, 1961.

I remember sitting on: Carolyn Pertwee, interview with author, February 16, 2013.

It was horrible, really: Ibid.

He taught me more about: Funke and Booth, *Actors talk About Acting*, 89.

When we would arrive: Coeks Gordon, interview with author, February 16, 2013.

a great one for writing: Carolyn Pertwee, interview with author, February 16, 2013.

forty years fell off her face: Vickers, *Vivien Leigh*, 295.

gained in reassurance: Elizabeth Reeve "The Old Vic on tour: An appraisal," publication unknown, Autumn-Winter 1962, vivien-leigh.com article database.

be greeted with applause: Eric Johns, "Vivien Leigh's World Tour," *Theatre World*, August 1961.

Could be simply enchanting: Mark Kingston and Marigold Sharman, interview for British Library Theatre Archive Project, March 31, 2006.

We got out of Rio: Jack Merivale, recorded memo for Anne Edwards, box 35, collection 1080, Anne Edwards Papers, UCLA (Los Angeles).

This is the age of: Vivien Leigh, "*Tovarich* Isn't *Aida*," *Philadelphia Enquirer Magazine*, January 13, 1963.

If anybody had told me: Wayne Robinson, "'Tovarich' Premieres Tomorrow," *Philadelphia Sunday Bulletin*, January 20, 1963.

felt good to be doing: Vivien Leigh, "I Gambled On a Musical," *Detroit Free Press*, date unknown, Theatre Collection clippings, New York Public Library (Manhattan).

You must not despair: Vivien Leigh, letter to Jack Merivale, December 28, 1962, Jack Merivale Papers, BFI Library (London).

Admittedly we did a marvelous: Ibid, January 27, 1963.

I should never have taken: Ibid, February 6, 1963.

I must confess to you: Ibid, March 11, 1963.

Thrilled and flattered: Rod Hall, "Vivien Leigh: My Girl Next Door," *Mail on Sunday*, January 12, 2003.

Just something I won: Ibid.

What's happening is that: John Gruen, *Close-up* (New York: The Viking Press, 1967), 22–23.

She had health problems: Stanley Kramer, interviewed for *Vivien Leigh: Scarlett and Beyond* (Turner Pictures, 1990)

Slipping and getting old: Mangan, *Gielgud Letters: John Gielgud in His Own Words*, 313.

terribly difficult: Ibid, 315.

She was no longer: Simon Signoret, *Nostalgia Isn't What It Used to Be* (New York: Harper & Row, 1978), 308.

extraordinary star, unsentimental: John Kobal, *Hollywood Color Portraits* (New York: Morrow, 1981), 44.

Realized that, in the picture: Stanley Kramer with Thomas M. Coffey, *A Mad, Mad, Mad, Mad World: A Life in Hollywood* (United States: Harcourt Brace, 1997), 208.

Legacy

Give us strength and gaiety: An Appreciation of Vivien Leigh: University of Southern California, March 17, 1968 (University of Southern California: Friends of the Libraries), 1969.

I am happy now: Robert Ottaway, "Vivien Leigh: The Mask Behind the Face," publication unknown, March 10, 1965.

the country, the outlook: Ottaway, "Vivien Leigh: The Mask Behind the Face."

Jack Merivale received letters: Vivien Leigh, letters to Jack Merivale, November 23– December 9, 1964, Jack Merivale Papers, BFI Library (London).

An Indian film: Ottaway, "Vivien Leigh: The Mask Behind the Face."

A sad piece of might-have-been: Dent, *Vivien Leigh: A Bouquet*, 175.

Oh, I've done all that: Ernest Schier, "Vivien Leigh: What is Undone Will Be Done." *Philadelphia Sunday Bulletin*, March 13, 1966.

The greatest beauty: *The Observer*, July 9, 1967.

exquisite actress, thoughtful, fearless: An Appreciation of Vivien Leigh: University of Southern California.

She always reminded me of: Noël Coward, *The Letters of Noël Coward (Diaries, Letters, and Essays)*. Barry Day, ed. (London: Methuen Drama, 2008), 747.

In December 1966: Dr. S. M. Whitteridge, letter to Laurence Olivier, Olivier Archive, British Library (London).

Olivier was diagnosed with: Binkie Beaumont, letter to Laurence Olivier, July 1967, Olivier Archive, British Library (London).

stood and prayed: Olivier, *Confessions of An Actor*, 290.

passionate devotion to: An Appreciation of Vivien Leigh: University of Southern California.

I hadn't seen them myself: George Cukor, letter to Gertrude Hartley, March 21, 1968, George Cukor Papers, AMPAS (Beverly Hills).

Vivien was wonderful on: Alec Guinness, interview with James Grissom, 1991.

It took the camera to: Kobal, *Hollywood Color Portraits*, 44.

truth is the keynote: Vivien Leigh, interviewed for *Small World* with Edward R. Murrow (CBS, December 1958).

PHOTO CREDITS

AMPAS: Pages 26 (top); 67; 86 (top); 93; 158 (top); 232

Author's Collection: Frontispiece; Pages 10; 16; 26 (bottom); 28; 29; 31; 47; 56; 69; 72; 73; 74; 79 (top left); 81; 86 (bottom-right); 88; 90; 91 (right); 102; 104 (bottom right); 110; 112; 117 (bottom); 126; 127; 130; 148; 149; 151; 157; 171; 172; 173; 190; 191; 192; 195; 198 (top); 199; 208; 240; 241 (top right, bottom)

British Library: Pages 18; 19

Carolyn Pertwee Collection: Pages 204; 217; 218 (bottom); 220

Courtesy of Dale McCarthy: Page 245

Debra Duncan Collection: Page 114 (top); 115 (bottom); 116; 117 (top)

Harvard Theatre Collection, Houghton Library, Harvard University: Pages 27 (top); 38; 39; 44; 92; 100; 119; 123; 124; 146; 152; 153; 154; 167; 168; 170; 179; 181; 182; 183; 184; 219; 236; 244

Hester St. John-Ives Collection: Pages 198 (left); 209; 222

Hulton Archive/Getty: Page 242

Independent Visions: Pages 15; 27 (bottom); 35; 46; 50; 51; 57; 58 (top, middle); 63; 65; 70; 75; 76; 77; 78 (bottom); 79 (middle, bottom); 80 (top); 83; 86 (bottom left); 91 (left); 106; 107; 109 (top); 113 (right); 121; 128; 129 (right); 132; 133 (bottom); 134; 135; 136; 140; 150 (top); 156; 158 (bottom); 163; 165; 174; 176; 177; 178; 186 (right); 187; 188 (left); 193; 197; 202; 206; 214; 216 (left); 223; 224; 235

Jay Jorgensen Collection: Pages 40; 48; 49; 53; 68; 78 (top); 108 (bottom); 131; 185; 213

Jonathan Frewen Collection: Pages 32; 33

Library of the London School of Economics and Political Science: Pages 94; 95

Marcus Adams Estate: Page 20

Mark Mayes Collection: Pages 8; 34; 32 (left, middle, center); 55 (bottom); 84 (right); 85 (top left, top right, bottom); 87; 98 (right, left); 246

Marguerite C. Collection: Pages 58 (bottom); 99; 138

NC Aventales AG (by permission of Alan Brodie Representation Ltd): Page 201

Nikki Luebke Collection: Page 54

Philippe Halsman Estate: Page 108

Popperfoto/Getty: Page 25

Private Collection: Pages 22; 180; 84 (left); 210; 218 (top); 221; 226; 241 (top left)

Private Collection: Pages 24; 36; 43; 59; 61; 62; 104 (bottom left); 113 (left); 160; 164; 175; 189; 211; 215; 216 (right); 227; 229; 231; 239

Richard Mangan Collection: Pages 80 (bottom); 104 (top left, right); 105; 174 (middle, bottom); 175 (top); 150 (bottom); 186 (left); 188 (right); 196

Sutterstock © Dubova p. 5, Fears p. 16, Markovka p. 44, tukkki p 70, Curly Pat p. 100, leziles p. 124, 168, Allydesign p. 146, 204

Sylwia Strepiak Collection: Pages 55 (top); 82; 133 (top); 139; 142; 143; 144; 194; 200; 212; 223 (left); 225; 207;

Trader Faulkner Collection: Pages 103; 162

INDEX